THE HAAS SISTERS
OF FRANKLIN STREET

THE HAAS SISTERS
OF FRANKLIN STREET

A SAN FRANCISCO MEMOIR OF FAMILY AND LOVE

FRANCES BRANSTEN ROTHMANN
FOREWORD BY KEVIN STARR

HEYDAY, BERKELEY, CALIFORNIA
SAN FRANCISCO HERITAGE, SAN FRANCISCO, CALIFORNIA

Library of Congress Cataloging-in-Publication Data is available.

Cover Photo and Page 114: jimsimmonsphotography.com

Chapter Opening Photos: Jody Stuart

Book Design: Ashley Ingram

Orders, inquiries, and correspondence should be addressed to:

Heyday

P.O. Box 9145, Berkeley, CA 94709

(510) 549-3564, Fax (510) 549-1889

www.heydaybooks.com

Printed in East Peoria, IL, by Versa Press, Inc.

10 9 8 7 6 5 4 3 2 1

To my mother, Florine Haas Bransten, to my aunt, Alice Haas Lilienthal, remembered with love; for my children, grandchildren, and succeeding generations so that they may enjoy and perpetuate these memories of the sisters.

Thanks to Professor Barth Marshall of the Fromm Institute and members of the family who shared their recollections and contributed so much to making this book a reality. Thanks to Susan and Léo Abrami, Alice and George Block, Sue and William Bransten, Cathryn and Edward Bransten, Elizabeth and James Gerstley, Claire and Ernest Lilienthal, John Rothmann, Madeleine Haas Russell, Frances and Laurence Stein, Haas Brothers, and M. J. B. Company for photographs.

—F.B.R., 1979

*

Acknowledgments for the 2017 edition: Alice Russell-Shapiro, John Rothmann, Susan Rothmann Seeley, and William Rothmann. Malcolm Margolin, Gayle Wattawa, and Steve Wasserman of Heyday. Special thanks to Mike Buhler, Terri Le, and Emma Doctors of San Francisco Heritage.

CONTENTS

FOREWORD

Kevin Starr

(1940–2017)

This vividly written memoir lovingly explores themes of family, sisterhood, the passage of years, and life among immigrant German Jewish San Franciscans who had succeeded, in terms of the American Dream, in the second half of the nineteenth and first half of the twentieth century. Centered on the sisters, Alice Haas Lilienthal and Florine Haas Bransten, the memoir evokes the mid- and late-nineteenth-century role played by German Jews in the creation of a great city through commerce and a sense of civilization brought over from Europe and reinforced by Jewish identity. It is also the autobiography of its author, Frances Bransten Rothmann, one of four children of Florine and her husband Edward Bransten.

On one level this is clearly a story of privileged families living in grand Victorians on Franklin Street: houses that have survived to this day and whose architectural exuberance and capaciousness continue to delight architectural historians and preservationists. In these grand and welcoming rooms, three generations experienced more than seventy years of marriages, births, child-rearing, and holiday celebrations that filled oversized first-level ballrooms with more than fifty relatives seated at ingeniously decorated tables, as well as more sedate Sunday-evening dinners that on a regular basis brought members of the extended

Haas, Greenebaum, Triest, Bransten, and Lilienthal families together at a great table in the comfort of the dining room with its richly paneled walls and coffered ceiling. It is also the continuing story of Frances Bransten Rothmann through childhood, adolescence, young adulthood, college at Barnard in New York, a romance there with a distinguished German physician, Hans Rothmann, followed by marriage and motherhood and the rearing of her own fourth-generation San Francisco family. Yes, San Francisco! For this memoir is as well a loving and detailed evocation of the city and what was achieved in the nineteenth century, destroyed by earthquake and fire in April 1906, then rebuilt, recapturing its unique existence as a world city on a human scale.

From this perspective, Rothmann centers her story on 2007 Franklin Street, where the Haas sisters, her mother and aunt, orchestrated the delightful pageant of family life that represented their existence. The narrative moves seamlessly to the nearby downtown where the sisters shopped so avidly in elegant department stores, took lunch or tea at the Garden Court of the Palace Hotel, caught a play at the Alcazar Theatre, or treated young Frances at Blum's to the most delicious ice cream and cake.

The Haas Sisters constitutes a love song to San Francisco past and present. "Present" because the two homes on Franklin Street have survived and in their later years continue to nurture daily life as only homes can do. Their daily life in San Francisco, as these pages reveal, emanated a mood of well-being—of being safe and at home amid the family in a city that fused the necessary and the practical with the poetry and deeper resonances, magic, even, of developed urban culture in a dramatic setting.

The narrative moves down the Peninsula to the Haas summer home in Atherton, with its vegetable gardens, tennis court, swimming pool, and greensward on which tables could be aligned for alfresco lunches in the sunshine that was so conspicuously absent on

Franklin Street during the fog-ridden San Francisco summer. Roth-mann deftly chronicles excursions to yet another summer home in a completely different direction: a popular resort on the shores of Lake Tahoe. The conjoined families—with more and more children added to their ranks as the years went on—traveled to Tahoe by standard- and narrow-gauge railroad. Over time, this arc of travel centered on Franklin Street would be extended to embrace New York and Europe to the east, Hawaii and Hong Kong across the Pacific, as the sisters and other family members became world travelers.

Here was a world of graciousness, family love, and leisure sufficient to allow the sisters time for five to six telephone calls a day to discuss a myriad of topics: budding romances of grown-up daughters and sons, forthcoming holidays, weddings celebrated on the great lawn at Ather-ton, menus for dinners to be ordered by telephone from a grocer who delivered, along with a milkman, a baker, and a dry cleaner who also delivered, and an aged family physician who made house calls.

Across their long lifetimes, Alice Haas Lilienthal and Florine Haas Bransten shared an enduring treasure of love, sisterhood, and friend-ship that formed the emotional and ceremonial nucleus of the larger family clan. Whatever happened—including the destruction of the city by earthquake and a fire that came within a block of destroying Franklin Street—whatever surprising developments might occur as the twentieth century progressed, there were always the sisters, the special delight, the secrets even, the smiles and mutual support they shared, the love and warmth, the regard for others that emanated outward as a matrix of identity and support for the entire clan.

Between 1904 and 1908, the first generation of the family returned to Germany to visit birthplaces, hometowns, and family relatives whom in earlier times decided not to emigrate to the United States. Fast-forward to World War II, when so many relatives, including Frances's husband, brother, and cousin, were serving in the armed forces. She, her mother, and her aunt rolled bandages for the Red Cross, served coffee and donuts to departing troops, invited assorted soldiers and sailors to holiday dinners, wrapped care packages, and wrote Victory letters: all this added to their continuing work with various Jewish charities keyed to the war effort.

During these years—from 1933 onward—a horror beyond imagination was being carried out against the Jews living in Europe, beginning in Germany, where the ancestors of these and all the other names in this San Francisco narrative had developed their personal, professional, and cultural identities. With great delicacy and restraint, Rothmann movingly concludes her narrative, written at the end of her long and happy life, probing the meaning of the distance between the German Jewish San Francisco of her narrative and the horrors of the Holocaust.

German Jews had played a major role in founding the city and bringing it to maturity. On Franklin Street, family members celebrated Christmas and Easter as secular American holidays, along with Thanksgiving and the Fourth of July, as well as special days in the Jewish calendar of observance at Temple Emanu-El.

The terrible events, the monstrous crimes in Europe of the 1930s and first half of the 1940s, obliged Rothmann to wrestle with questions that could never be answered. "For Mother's and Aunt Alice's particular class of Jew in San Francisco," Rothmann writes, "the nineteenth century was one of security, propriety, tranquility: one of successful enterprises, affluence, and social amenities....What could they know of ghettos, iron-fisted militarism, and revolutions that existed for their forefathers a century earlier? What could they know of persecution, these ladies who were so loved and accepted? How could they smell the horror of the ashes of their fellow Jews, thousands of miles removed from isolated San Francisco? The daggers of pain and death could not penetrate their senses, but their hearts were never immune to the suffering of others."

As a fourth-generation San Franciscan who lives on Franklin Street just two blocks away from where the sisters lived, I appreciate this memoir and the San Francisco these families helped to create.

Two Victorian Sisters

◇◇

Once upon a time, in the long-ago 1880s, San Francisco's Franklin Street was a fashionable residential district. On this street, within the distance of three blocks bounded by California and Jackson Streets, lived three married Greenebaum sisters. These women, my grandmother and two great-aunts, lived out their stately, orderly lives in spacious Victorian mansions. Today, Franklin Street is a busy one-way thoroughfare. The houses of my great-aunts, Carrie Walter and Stella Simon, were demolished and replaced by stucco apartment buildings. But two family homes remain on Franklin Street. The one at 2007 Franklin Street was built for my grandparents, Bertha and William Haas, in 1886; it is a tall, gray Victorian with turrets, bay windows, intricate carvings, and a Queen Anne tower. The other, at 1735 Franklin Street and built in 1904, is a red brick, ivy-covered Georgian from the Edwardian period with imposing white pillars. This house was a wedding gift to my parents from my grandparents.

I was born there in 1914, the youngest of four children. At that time, it was customary for babies to be delivered at home and for female relatives to attend the birth. Aunt Alice was present when our myopic, elderly family doctor brought me into the world. The doctor, a close friend and physician for the entire clique of Franklin

Street dwellers, tended Mother during her labor. When I arrived, he proclaimed triumphantly, "Florine, darling, you have a lovely little boy." Aunt Alice, modest and innocent as she was, timidly cleared her throat in contradiction. "Dear doctor, if you will glance farther down at baby, I think you will see that you are looking at the umbilical cord. The baby, I believe, is a little girl."

As a child I could roller-skate, bicycle ride, and play on safe, quiet Franklin Street. I could climb on the back of the iceman's truck, grab the icicles that melted off the blocks of ice, and suck happily on them. I could rush down the street to greet the knife sharpener as he came on foot with his grinding wheel, and I could meet the old man who cried, "Rags, bottles, sacks," as he ambled by with his horse and buggy. I could dash across the street to watch the organ-grinder perform with a trained monkey who was dressed up in a saucy hat and red jacket and was dexterous at collecting pennies. I could play in the big vacant sandlot on the other side of the house, where two apartment buildings now stand. In that lot, playing with forbidden matches, my sister Alice and cousin Liz started a roaring bonfire that nearly ignited the neighborhood.

My mother, Florine, often called "Lorlie," and my Aunt Alice, and my uncle, Charles, grew up in the Victorian house. Uncle Charlie died in his early forties; his sisters outlived him by half a century. Mother and Aunt Alice were married in the drawing rooms of 2007 Franklin, my grandfather's house. Shortly after their wedding, Mother and Father moved to the Edwardian Georgian down the street. When Alice married Sam Lilienthal, they lived on Gough Street for a short while; after my grandfather's death, however, they moved into the Victorian to live with my grandmother.

Throughout their long lives, Mother and Aunt Alice, three and a half years apart in age, remained devoted to each other. After they married, they lived less than four blocks apart and visited back and forth constantly, and phoned each other several times a day. They exchanged Sunday and holiday dinners, fussing compulsively as to menus, decor, and seating for each of these gatherings as though they were entertaining royalty. They walked downtown via Sutter Street (which they pronounced "Sooter," the German way; also Kearny was "Carney," the Irish way) to shop, to exercise, and to accomplish many mysterious errands. All along the route, they either had fits of giggles over some inanity amusing only to themselves or they scolded one another over a minor infraction. Their progress was often delayed by the conniptions that doubled them over in paroxisms of laughter, or by what they called "unbelievable behavior," which left them either fuming in immobility or stalking away in the wrong direction.

The sisters thought no evil of anyone, and tended to love or humor everyone with whom they had contact, but each was capable of incensing the other. If one sister were preoccupied or busy in her private life, it would seem to the other that she had been neglected or excluded. "All Florine thinks about is Ed. She spoils her husband and leaves no time for herself," was a polite way of saying, "There is no time for me." From time to time, Mother was miffed when her sister spent too much time playing cards with other cronies, but forgiveness came as quickly as flare-ups.

Florine and Alice made a life out of thinking of others and devoted their attentions to arranging celebrations, shopping for gifts, and planning surprises for a butcher, a seamstress, an old relative, a sick child—anyone and everyone whose services or feelings they valued. They found everyone charming and lovable; their indiscriminate belief and trust were capable of transforming a mean scoundrel into a generous, kind soul. People wished to live up to their endearing confidence and affection.

One day the two sisters dared to drive to Oakland bent on some obscure "important" errand. Chatting merrily, absorbed in each other rather than their route, they took the DO NOT ENTER ramp on the bridge. A compassionate truck driver spotted their plight and rushed to their rescue, offering to turn their car safely around and onto the right ramp. So enormous was their relief that they immediately insisted, "Come along, young fellow, we want to take you to lunch!" What an unusual threesome they must have been!

Another day, they again ventured to drive across the Bay Bridge. Characteristically, the sisters had chosen to patronize a tailor in the East Bay rather than go to one more conveniently located. As usual, they were so absorbed in conversation that they lost their way in Oakland. They flagged down a truck and the driver obligingly guided them to the tailor's very door. Of course, they took him to lunch. Another day, when Aunt Alice was chauffeuring Mother in Palo Alto, her ancient Cadillac stalled in the middle of a busy street. Mother, understandably frightened, scolded her furiously, "For goodness sake, Alice, don't stop in the middle of traffic. At least pull over to the curb." "Can't you see that I can't? The car won't move! Do you think I'm doing this on purpose?" Aunt Alice fumed. A policeman cycled to their rescue and escorted them out of the way of the flow of oncoming automobiles. Their gratitude welled over. "My, but you are smart. How did you manage to start up the car? You're an angel, and if you will just follow us, we want to buy you an ice-cream cone." The officer explained, "You must see, ladies, it's quite impossible to manage a cone on a motorcycle, nor would it really be right for an officer in uniform to go licking away." Mother and Aunt Alice were so persistent in their gratitude that they finally got his home address and promptly sent him a large box of Blum's best chocolates.

On another day, the sisters ventured off in Mother's cumbersome old Marmon. Mother had learned to drive quite late in life and had never mastered it properly. She zigzagged and stalled the car on a hill and was finally flagged down by a policeman who demanded to see her license. With her customary graciousness and warmth, Mother exclaimed gratefully, "Oh, policeman dearie, I'm so glad that you stopped me. Do you know I'd have driven all the way down to Atherton without my license? I left it in the top bureau drawer—the left side of that chiffonier my gloves are in. Now if you'll just help me turn around on this horrible hill, I'll hurry back and get my license."

One afternoon Mother was frantically searching her home from the attic to the basement. It seemed she was in desperate need of a dinner bell. I wondered about this because she had a buzzer with a fine tone in her dining room. Her explanation was, "I must find a loud clanging extra bell. I know I had one. The horn on the automobile is out of order and I must drive Aunt Alice to market right away. She can open her window and lean out and ring the bell until I get the horn repaired."

I have often laughed at Mother's innocent recountings and wondered how the sisters wriggled out of dire situations, but I have never heard a finale to their many tales. I do know that my mother's license was finally and blessedly revoked. Although her pride was offended, she said, "Those license people are so nice, I'm going to shop for a special gift to present to them, so that they'll know I harbor no hard feelings." Mother was actually relieved. She was quite ready to relinquish the wheel after she rammed into some shrubs, knocked them over, and got stuck in a ditch. At no time, however, was she ever ready to relinquish her backseat driving, which was notorious. As a passenger driving up a steep San Francisco hill, she assisted the driver by leaning forward in order that the car shouldn't topple over, convinced that her own light weight could influence the powerful machine. She would gasp with fright, grit her teeth, and sit rigidly, no matter who chauffeured her.

Top: 2007 Franklin Street This gray Victorian was built for William and Bertha Haas in 1886, as designed by San Francisco architect Peter R. Schmidt. Daughter Alice Haas was reared here, and after her father's death, in 1916, Alice and her husband, Samuel, moved into the house to live with her widowed mother. Alice lived here until her death, in 1972, three blocks from her sister. Today the house is a museum, open to the public, also housing the offices of San Francisco Heritage.
Bottom: 1735 Franklin Street The red-brick home of Edward and Florine Bransten was designed by San Francisco architect Herman Barth and built in 1904. It was a wedding gift from the bride's family, survived the earthquake in 1906, and is still a private residence.

Opposite page, top: left to right: Alice, William Haas, Charles, Florine, Bertha Haas, and nephew Louis Greene, circa 1889. **Middle left:** Alice Haas Lilienthal, 1930s. **Middle right:** Florine Haas Bransten, circa 1940. **Bottom left:** Alice Haas Lilienthal and daughter Elizabeth, born 1913. **Bottom right, top:** The Bransten family sedan, circa 1920. **Bottom right:** The dining room at 2007 Franklin Street, 1960.

SUNDAY DINNERS, HOLIDAYS, FESTIVALS, SPECIAL OCCASIONS

◇◇◇

Sunday dinner was a weekly ritual. The tradition began when my grandmother and grandfather were alive, and it continued for another sixty years until my mother and Aunt Alice had both died. It was not unusual for twenty or more persons to be gathered around Aunt Alice's extended oak table or my mother's walnut one. Each Sunday's menu, decor, and seating had to be original and varied. The sisters vied with each other over what to serve and how to decorate. Seating became a major strategic puzzle, even if everyone present was related. At times my mother would entrust me with this fortnightly problem. These occasions invariably included discussion over favorite dishes, digestion, and whom to please. Once, I went shopping with Mother, who, toting a pink candle, hurried to Blum's to find matching candies and then rushed on to the florist for a pink arrangement. The question of floral shades and contrasts assumed world-shaking proportions. Holiday dinners were exchanged as well as Sunday dinners. Aunt Alice was designated the Christmas hostess; Mother was the Thanksgiving hostess; Easter depended on whose turn it was to host for that week. Every occasion and holiday was shared and fashioned into a cause célèbre.

Aunt Alice's Christmas Eve will always be a high point in my memories. I can still smell the fragrant aroma of fir and pine boughs in the crackling fire. I can still sense the excitement and anticipation as we viewed the elaborately wrapped gifts glowing in their incandescent papers, bows, and promises of wishes fulfilled. I can see the sparkle of tinsel and lights. I can hear the rustle of evening dresses, the hum of expectation, and the whispering of excited children.

Preparation for the Christmas party started many months earlier. As Aunt Alice's daughters grew up, they were enlisted as her aides. For days on end they would be closeted behind locked doors, deep in secret schemes. Aunt Alice seemed to be Mrs. Santa Claus personified; her daughters, elfin helpers. With the passage of time, the family multiplied. When our Christmas gatherings grew to include between fifty and sixty cousins, sisters, uncles and aunts, the party was transferred from the warmth of upstairs parlors and dining room to the bare and colder regions of the basement ballroom. This large room, with its slippery hardwood floors, echoing walls, and gas fixtures, had a small elevated platform at one end upon which stood a tall looking glass that seemed to elongate the room. These chilly, subterranean depths were transformed into other worlds. Each year there was a new stage-setting, a new burst of imagination, and infinite attention to detail. One Christmas, the guests were magically transplanted to Mexico. Santa Claus piñatas dangled from gas fixtures, while colorful sombreros, Indian baskets, papier-mâché chickens and horses, and full-blown paper poppies decorated the long dining tables. In a scramble of merriment, gleeful children whacked noisily at the Santa piñatas and were showered with small gifts and candies.

Another Christmas, the ballroom became a scene from the Orient. Several of the ladies wore kimonos Aunt Alice had brought home from the Far East, where she explored shops more thoroughly than historical landmarks. It was a "must" to forage out gifts for long lists of family and friends; gifts were as essential to Alice and Florine as breathing or sleeping. This evening, Siamese silver and gold wind-bells chimed merrily, Japanese paper butterflies and fans revealed their vibrant colors, and Hong Kong lanterns, shaped as odd animals, lit the tables. My favorite Christmas scenes were those in which the old house became a winter wonderland and Santa's North Pole was reproduced. Once, Aunt Alice constructed trees out of silvered pine-cones that she had carefully gathered the previous summer in Tahoe. They were festooned with popcorn and shining ornaments, all labori-ously threaded. Each guest received an Alice-knitted washrag, balled into the shape of fruits and liberally sprinkled with spangles. Another Christmas, every lady received red velvet shoe trees fashioned into Santas. A miniature replica of winter in the Alps served as the buffet table's centerpiece. An ice-skating pond, surrounded by snow-laden, stubby bushes was designed on a long, flat mirror. Within the center of a miniature forest stood a gingerbread chalet, which had been fash-ioned by the able hands of the devoted cook. Tiny toboggans, sleds, shimmering paper snowballs, and a roly-poly Santa balancing on top of the chalet's chimney sparkled their reflections on the mirror-pond. Another Christmas dinner's centerpiece featured a plump suckling pig with a shining red apple protruding under its snout. It was gar-landed with holly and gloriously glazed, but it would never grace the table again. Despite the fact that it was festive to behold and aromatic to sniff, it was too sinewy to be as delightfully edible as it appeared to be; it had failed perfection.

Every Christmas, either in the windowed alcove of the second par-lor, fronting on Franklin Street, or on the platform in the ballroom, a ceiling-high tree shone as it revolved slowly on a music stand and exuded the heady fragrance of fir. Its sturdy, amazingly symmetrical branches were heavily weighted with heirloom ornaments, ropes of shining tinsel, and blinking multitudes of lights. The secret of those thick symmetrical branches became known to me in time: Aunt Alice had extra boughs cemented to the tree's trunk whenever it was not perfectly proportioned. Through the sheer force of her own persuasive enthusiasm, Aunt Alice was able to inveigle someone to hoist himself into a Santa Claus suit stuffed with pillows, invent a suitable patter, disguise his voice, and perform generally uncomfortable antics for enchanted small-fry. Before dinner, in the upstairs parlor where adults imbibed cocktails and ate holiday hors d'oeuvres, Santa would come bounding down the stairs with a rush of sleigh bells and roaring belly laughs. For several years in a row, Aunt Alice secured an enthusiastic Santa—a towering family friend who loved children, enjoyed performing, and had a great imagination. George was Santa Claus when my youngest child was six. I was as thrilled to Christmas magic through my son's shining eyes as I had been years earlier when I was a believing toddler. John was mystified by Santa's ingenuity, agog that what was requested from Santa before dinner was granted immediately afterwards. How hard it would have been for a child to sit through the Christmas feast had it not been for the fanciful favors, surprise settings, and small gifts Santa distributed at his grand entrance—for no one was allowed to touch the enticingly stacked packages until the last dinner crumb was cleared away.

After my husband and I flew to Copenhagen via the North Pole in 1955, we told John we had waved to Santa. The following Christmas, Aunt Alice's inventive "George-Claus" corroborated our story, relating to John that he had seen Mommie and Daddy and waved back to them as the plane passed over his house. Mommie, he assured John, had let notes carrying his Christmas wishes flutter down directly to him through the falling snow. Little John was marvelously impressed by this story and so his belief in Santa Claus continued. Christmas Eve did not end the celebration. In early years, Alice and Florine sewed and stitched giant Christmas stockings that looked more like Santa *sacks* than stockings. They were distributed on the twenty-fourth, hung over the fireplaces—bulging with manifold gifts—and ready for the children when they awakened on the twenty-fifth. This tradition eased the goodnights and facilitated the finale of the pageantry. There was much to look forward to in the morning if one hurried to bed.

New Year's Eve was generally a quiet affair. However, one New Year's Eve proved to be far from sedate. Cruising on a transatlantic steamer trip, Mother had been enchanted with the puffballs the passengers used to celebrate the occasion in the ship's lounge. She approached the purser beguilingly. "Dearie, my grandchildren would just love those soft cotton-like balls you used at that marvelous party last night. They could throw them and no one could get hurt. Do you think you could possibly spare a few bags for me to take home?" The purser was charmed by Mother's enthusiasm, and she returned home triumphantly bearing several bags of puffballs, which the children boisterously tossed back and forth over the dinner table. After the elaborate meal, my parents, Aunt Alice, and Uncle Sam dutifully propped their eyes open, stifled yawns, and chatted with determination until the stroke of midnight, when ceremoniously they opened champagne, exchanged good wishes, and with sighs of relief, bade each other goodnight.

Easter brings memories of the rainbow colors of a pastel wonderland. To this day, I can sense the excitement of scrambling around a lawn, thrusting my hand into shrubs and bushes searching frantically for hidden eggs. Each child was given a basket tied up in fancy ribbons. Some baskets were more elaborate than others, and one coveted the prettiest. Hunts took place at either of the sisters' homes, in their front gardens, which faced Franklin Street. No wonder passersby stopped to gape. When I grew older, I discovered the secret of those prolonged hunts: the older children sneaked eggs out of the younger ones' baskets and re-hid them, so that Florine and Alice could continue to enjoy this happy contest from their box seats at the windows. Their conspiracy gave pleasure to everyone. The one who found the most eggs won a prize. This was usually an oversized crystalized sugar egg garlanded with vines and roses. When held up to the light, one could peer through a tiny hole and see miniature figures and trees. I never won the prize, but, inasmuch as the egg was not edible, I never felt too badly. After the hunt, we settled down to picnic lunches and munched both hard-boiled eggs and lush chocolate ones, gluey with marshmallow. These noon picnics did not preclude the Sunday Easter dinners, for which the ladies dressed in long, flowing chiffons, looking like spring incarnate. Bouquets of yellow and pink tulips, soft blue iris, rosy anemones, and ranunculus mingled with rainbow shades of candles. These flickered their myriad colors down the entire length of the elongated table. As a child, I was permitted to assist in Easter preparations. My mother or Aunt Alice would give a dipping-dyeing party the day before the event. I was the clumsiest of all the bunny-helpers and invariably spilled the saucers of colored dye on my dress and on the carpet. My cousin Liz was marvelously adept. She could puncture a fragile raw egg and blow out its contents, a feat I never achieved. The eggs Liz dyed were by far the most beautiful. No wonder she later became Santa Claus's helper!

July Fourth was a blaze of glory, a vivid medley of red, white, and blue flags and firecrackers. Every summer my aunt and uncle moved to the country home in Atherton, thirty miles south of San Francisco. On Independence Day, the spacious grounds resounded with the voices of every age group, with the pong of tennis balls, bicycles and horses crunching over gravel paths, and the happy shrieks and splashes of swimmers. The festive dinner was preceded by a long, lovely afternoon of sunbathing, tennis, and swimming. Aunt Alice and Mother would glide up and down the "swimming tank," as they called the pool, in rhythmic breaststroke with heads high above the water, chatting away as if they were strolling. They were modestly dressed in knee-length black bathing suits and long black stockings. Once out of the pool, they wrapped themselves in big absorbent towels and hurried to change into pale print dresses, brimmed straw hats, and white kid shoes. Settling out of the sun, they would sit and knit, clicking and clucking, giggling and scolding, all the while observing everyone and everything from their shaded posts. As dusk fell, the long redwood tables would be set in resplendent patriotic colors. The smaller children were given sparklers. It was fearfully exciting to go running around the circular plot of grass, carrying what seemed to me a lighted torch. I was afraid of its fiery flare, but I was also intrigued by its sparkling crackle. The buffet table would suddenly be crowded with freshly picked corn on the cob, oozing butter, crisp salads, browned chickens, and marbled cheeses. All this was crowned later by homemade berry ice cream and thickly fudged chocolate cake. I have never tasted ice cream that measured up to the essence of those garden-gathered blackberries laden with rich cream, nor has anyone ever been able to duplicate the cake that was lush with gleaming black frosting. When the sky inked out and the clatter of cutlery had settled, the gardener, accompanied by the privileged older boys, retreated to a safe distance to light rockets and firecrackers. The sky lit up with multicolored brilliant flares and the garden shuddered and gasped with loud bangs. Throughout this spectacular show, Alice and Florine clutched their ears, recoiling from the explosions. Although they both detested this annual noisy performance, they would not dream of depriving us of our celebration.

Crimson and gold chrysanthemums and autumn leaves were massed in the center of Mother's dining-room table for Thanksgiving. Daylong aromas of roasting and baking filled the house with anticipation. The evening's gathering meant another party and another mingling with cousins. I can still hear the grating of Father's carving knife as he whipped it across the sharpening stone, poised above the huge bronzed turkey. He smiled inquiringly, "White or dark?" Many Thanksgivings fuse into a medley of sensual impressions, but the one I recall in particular was when I was about twelve years old. My cousins and I decided to act out a Thanksgiving play. Our decision entailed much whispering, giggling, and shoving and nudging before the imaginary curtain rose. At that age I constantly inflicted a performance on anyone I could. The best audiences were Aunt Alice and Mother, who patiently waited through the snickers and wiggles and applauded enthusiastically at whatever was produced. "Just marvelous," they laughed in uproarious appreciation. I usually composed, directed, and then assigned myself the leading role in every drama. The center of the stage so transported me that I never considered my cousins; I just shoved them about like puppets. Aunt Alice affectionately came to nickname me "The Oh and Ah Fairy" because my favorite role was that of a fairy godmother who arrived out of nowhere to bring happiness and fulfill wishes with one stroke of her wand. While performing magic feats, the fairy godmother's ecstatic chant was "Oh," followed by a long, drawn-out "Ahhh." Thanks to our chiffonier in the playroom of the attic, which had drawers filled with costumes, I was able to outfit myself as a Puritan maid with a huge poke bonnet, severe grey dress, and tidy white apron. I was actually a fairy disguised as a Puritan who bestowed a Thanksgiving feast on snowbound sufferers starving in a desolate and barren New England kitchen. After this play, my cousins rebelled. The only lines allotted to them were a few mumbled, "Thank you, fairy godmother," and "Thank you, God." They protested that for the next production they would compose, direct, and play the leads. Aside from my shocked surprise at their mutiny that evening, I recall the large "book" my mother placed in the center of the table, amidst a cluster of leaves. Inscribed in large brown letters on its red wooden binding was the title *By Branstens-Lilienthals— Pantry Poems. Limited Holiday Edition—Hunger and Thirst Grublishers.*

After dinner the book was opened. We were astonished to find that it was a hollow box; in place of pages, packages were neatly tied up in paper and ribbons. A "Florine Godmother" had worked her magic. Perhaps Mother was getting even with her sister and wished to rival Aunt Alice's Christmas beneficence; whatever the case, the loot proved disappointing to me. The prizes were mostly small kitchen utensils such as strainers or measuring spoons, packages of sugar crystals, vanilla beans, cinnamon sticks, or hoarded recipes inveigled from a miserly aunt, usually reluctant to reveal such secrets. I had hoped for jacks or skip-ropes. Fifty years later, my younger son John spotted this wooden book-box displayed in the window of a second-hand store. He triumphantly purchased it as a souvenir of his roots and of an era of very long ago, when his grandmother and great-aunt conjured up their original, decorative props for holidays.

There was no holiday that did not provide the sisters with an excuse to give a gift. On Valentine's Day, a chocolate heart, an embroidered handkerchief, or some such frilled token, mysteriously signed. On Halloween, a candy-filled pumpkin, all-day suckers fashioned into witches and ghosts—whatever could be conjured up that was appropriate. The only special day they rejected was Mother's Day. They always preferred to give rather than receive—a characteristic that could be irritating at times. "Please don't spend your good money on me" was a "Mother Maxim." They were as embarrassed by gifts as they were by compliments, both of which they loved to bestow on others. They protested that Mother's Day was a commercial invention; with shy reluctance, they accepted only a handpicked bouquet from their own gardens, an original poem, or some such homemade present. In later years, they nimbly contradicted themselves by giving their daughters a special memento on Mother's Day. Their rationalization was that their daughters had mothered their darling grandchildren.

Top left: Frances Lilienthal ready for an Easter-egg hunt, 1928. Top right: Easter-egg hunt on the lawn of 2007 Franklin Street, circa 1908. In the foreground, Alice Haas helps a youngster count the eggs. Middle left, top: Elizabeth Lilienthal Gerstley's Christmas Parties album documents the family's annual holiday gatherings at 2007 Franklin Street between 1954 and 1971. Middle left, bottom: "Branstens-Lilienthals—Pantry Poems. Limited Holiday Edition—Hunger and Thirst Grublishers." Each year, Florine filled the hollow wooden box masquerading as a book with sundry gifts neatly tied up in paper and ribbons. Middle center: Holiday-bedecked ballroom at 2007 Franklin Street, Christmas 1961. Middle right: Holiday time, 1964. Sisters Florine, left, and Alice dressed in holiday colors; one wore green, the other red. Bottom left: Frances Lilienthal Stein and daughter Judith in kimonos at 2007 Franklin Street, 1960.

Top left: "Pine Brook," the family's country home in Atherton, in 2000. Built in 1914, the cultivated twelve-acre estate, with its Tudor-style buildings and lush gardens, was sold in 2011. (The property was acquired by Jacob Stern in 1906.) **Middle left:** The pool area at "Pine Brook," Atherton, 1960s. **Bottom left:** Parterre rose gardens, 1960s. **Top right:** Alice swimming at Atherton, 1940s. **Bottom right:** Alice swimming at Atherton, 1950s.

ALL IN AN AVERAGE DAY: THE TWENTIES

Every morning Mother rose early, unbraided her pigtails, brushed her hair vigorously, swirled it around on top of her head, and ferociously jabbed in tortoiseshell hairpins. After this ritual, she cleaned off her brush and pushed the collected hairs into a little linen pouch, securing the bag by its strings. This was to make a false hairpiece to match her own hair should it ever be needed. At 7:30 a.m., scrubbed and neat, smelling of castile soap, with a hand-crocheted bed jacket around her shoulders, she rang to have her coffee served in bed. Father would have been in the dining room a good hour earlier, reading the *Examiner* and the *Chronicle*. After Mother's breakfast, the cook would knock and a thirty-minute consultation would ensue as to luncheon and dinner menus, interrupted only by Father's perfunctory goodbye kiss to Mother's forehead. After the cook gathered her list, Mother began to telephone. Nothing entertained me more than eavesdropping on her calls, which were more on the order of monologues than dialogues. When I had any slight ailment, it was always called "grippe" and I was allowed to stay home from school and slide between the cool, slippery linen sheets on Father's adjoining twin bed and listen to Mother.

"Central, dearie, connect me with my sister. I hope I'm not too early. You know how she is; she doesn't like to have her coffee get cold. The number? It's East 87. Are you new? Allie, hello, dearie. I thought we should start our Christmas shopping. There's the nicest new Central. So helpful! I wonder what we could send her for Christmas. No, she didn't *sound* married. My Frances is home with grippe, so I want to attend to lemon drops, and I must buy some penny postcards and some two-cent stamps, and I should go to that nice Mr. Lazarus at the White House for two yards of ribbon; the children need hair ribbons. Miss Harder and Annie Quinn are coming this morning. All right, dearie, come for lunch, and we'll walk together." Bang went the receiver on its little black hook. Up it would go again as Mother jiggled the hook impatiently. "Central, dear, give me the butcher. Butcher, dearie, my sister is coming for lunch. What do you think she'd like? What did she have for lunch yesterday?" Mother never waited for an answer, but rattled on breathlessly: "I already gave Cook the order, but I think I'll change it to lamb chops. And tonight I'll have a *nice* roast beef. My Frances has the grippe, so she'll just have soft-boiled eggs." Bang, down went the telephone again. Once I ventured to ask, "How does the butcher know who you are, and how does Central know which butcher you want? You never state any names or how much meat you want." "Darling, that's dear Joe Hermann," Mother answered, as though that explained everything. Up went the phone again. "Hello, dearie, I'd like two dozen eggs and three pounds of butter." I thought it best not to ask who the "dear butter-and-egg man" was.

After her telephone sessions, Mother rose and reappeared in a Hoover apron. The apron was an enveloping white affair, a family uniform which had mysteriously derived its name from President Herbert Hoover. All the ladies of the household wore it when tidying bureau drawers, writing letters, and fixing flowers. Once a week, Miss Harder, a prim, gaunt spinster, knocked at the door. She appeared with her business-like valise filled with various brushes and curling irons to wash Mother's long hair in the big marble basin. A little later, Annie Quinn, the manicurist, might arrive and set out her equipment on the card table. While Mother's hair was towel dried and each of her nails carefully buffed, it was comforting to listen to the murmuring voices. About this time, Cecilia the upstairs maid would come in. It was her job to help Mother button herself into her tailored suit and collect the proper matching gloves, shoes, hat, and bag. Sometimes Mother extended her hand, gingerly holding out dollar bills, "Please, Cecilia, dearie, I'd like these washed and ironed. I hate touching this dirty stuff." I had often watched in amazement as Cecilia ironed paper dollars in the attic's sewing room. I am quite sure that the only reason Mother didn't have her silver dollars washed was that she collected them from the St. Francis Hotel, which had a special polishing machine just for this purpose. Mother had money laundered and ironed because she was inordinately fastidious. Everything had to look, feel, taste, and smell immaculate; nothing was to be soiled, dingy, rancid, or rough to the touch. I can see her seated at table, painstakingly peeling Muscat grapes and halving them to extract the seeds because she found the skin unpalatable and tough. Sniffing a pitcher of cream, she might cautiously pour a dollop on a spoon, taste and frown, puzzling over whether it was sufficiently sweet and fresh. Commenting on what she ate, she might shake her head dolefully, saying, "This has a very funny taste, don't you find?" Rarely could anyone else "find." When Mother dined in a hotel, train, or public place, she wiped the silver surreptitiously, so that no one could take offense.

Lunching downstairs on their frenched and frilled chops, Mother and Alice might haggle over something inconsequential. If they weren't bickering, they might be discussing the disposal of excess tickets for events of a charitable or civic nature, which might include Temple Emanu-El, the Policeman's Ball, the Fireman's Ball, the Opera, the Symphony, the Browning Society, or the World Affairs lectures. The sisters always had stacks of various tickets. When dessert was served and Aunt Alice claimed to be dieting, the waitress brought her a silver fruit knife and fork, a green apple, saccharin for her coffee, and a generous slice of freshly baked chocolate cake.

After carefully dipping their fingers in the finger bowls and assiduously blotting their mouths, the sisters sometimes left the house via the basement so that Mother could talk to Wah, the Chinese laundryman. When Mother went to the basement, she always raised her voice and spoke to Wah in "pidgin English." "You did very good laundry tablecloth. No put starch in mister's shirt." It seemed that Wah was with us forever. Only once did he leave for an extended period of time; he wanted to visit his wife in China before he died. Wah returned bearing bolts of silk for everyone and continued his life in the basement. I liked visiting Wah in the mysterious confines of the basement, but I was strictly forbidden to intrude on his private little room off the furnace area. Instead of joining the maids for meals, he sometimes devised his own concoctions on a gas burner. The odd-smelling foods he prepared sent their odors sailing through the house and the maids indignantly trotted about opening windows. Once I was permitted to go out to lunch in Chinatown with Wah. We sat on a balcony from which I watched pigtailed Chinese in black pantaloons and jackets scurrying along as they bore baskets on their bent shoulders. I loved the adventure and I loved Wah's kind, wizened face and gentle manner. When Wah ate in the kitchen, he sat in silence at a separate table from the chattering maids. I thought this discriminatory, sensing that he must feel lonely and unloved. At times when I begged, I was allowed to join him at his table; then we would both sit munching in silence. I remember very little spoken communication with Wah; perhaps he did not speak English very well. Wah carried my bicycle onto the street for me, and later he assisted me with baby carriages. Sometimes he grinned and proclaimed, "Once bicycle, now baby buggy!"

The house seemed sad and quiet when Mother and Alice were out. I listened to the hours as they struck on the big grandfather clock in the hall and counted eagerly for five booms. At five, Mother would ring the front doorbell (as one of the servants was always on duty) and came upstairs to bathe and dress for dinner. She usually telephoned Aunt Alice before bathing because there was always something she had overlooked, even though they had spent hours together that very day. Mother devoted a few afternoons to me, although I usually roller-skated, bicycled, or played with neighborhood children on the front lawn. When we were together, we might go to the seamstress, Mrs. Siem, who made children's clothes. Mrs. Siem lived "way out on Cherry Street," according to Mother. Fletcher, the chauffeur, had to drive us to her house in the limousine. For several years, Aunt Alice and Mother shared this convenient means of transportation— an inheritance from their mother, for Grandmother Haas had had Fletcher and the big black Pierce-Arrow for as many years as I can remember. Mother and Aunt Alice always worried and argued as to who was to take Fletcher that day, forever fearful of depriving each other. As they usually went out together, and mostly on foot, I never could fathom their turmoil. Mrs. Siem whipped up dresses for my cousins as well as for my sister and me. I had nothing to say about how my clothes should be designed, nor did I care. I thought the whole procedure tedious. Then, one day I was to get a new party dress. Up until then my party dresses were green or blue shapeless chiffons that looked the same in front as in back—so much so that I often put them on wrong way around. One of my classmates, Adelaide Brown, had a bright-yellow dress that fitted snugly across the top to reveal two uptilting points. At recess, all the boys collected around Adelaide, their eyes riveted on those points. I was sure that if I had a dress like Adelaide's, I'd look like her and the boys would flock around me, too. I tried to explain this dress to my mother, who smiled serenely, promising to describe it to Mrs. Siem. "Frances would like a yellow dress with a sash around it, dearie." Mother had not understood, so I tried to tell Mrs. Siem myself. She was rendered speechless and slithered around on her knees with pins in her mouth, adjusting my hem and nodding in cordial agreement. No one bothered to explain to me that I was not yet properly equipped. I still wore a "waist" (undershirt) to which my panties were buttoned, and over that I wore a flannel petticoat. I was obviously completely shapeless, and, sad to say, unfashionable. Mother and Aunt Alice had strict dictates as to how young girls should look: brassieres were considered as daring as vulgar lipstick. Neither sister ever used lipstick, a product only suitable for "painted, loose women."

Mother and Aunt Alice relied on sources other than Mrs. Siem to secure clothes for their daughters. During the eleven-year interval that Grandmother was a widow, she traveled abroad with her beloved right-hand maid and closest companion, Martha Ivanhoff. On their journeys, Grandmother and "Markie" shopped extensively for the grandchildren. Within the tissued layers of Grandmother's trunk drawers were the lovely treasures she had purchased in Europe. She brought back Liberty-print fine-cotton dresses from London, which were intricately hand smocked, unique and colorful in design. Even more exquisite were the pastel, accordion-pleated chiffons from Fairyland, the children's store in Paris. The dresses had soft "bertha" collars with matching satin bows on the shoulders. I remember wearing a pale-blue model that seemed to have been woven of gossamer. Then there was the New York City store De Pinna. Once a year their representative came to San Francisco for two weeks and set up shop at the Fairmont Hotel; orders could be given for any of the displayed merchandise. One unforgettable day, Mother and Aunt Alice actually decided to take their daughters shopping independently of one another. Several weeks later, Mother confessed excitedly to her sister, "My New York order has arrived. I must show you the beautiful coats I bought my girls." "How funny, Florine," Alice replied, "I, too, have lovely new coats to show you!" So we all met to admire our newly acquired finery. It was as if we were parading into a mirror. All of the cousins were there, decked out in the same model of De Pinna's reefer coats, navy blue with shining brass buttons.

Another afternoon, Mother might take me to "pay calls" on one of her aunts or uncles. If we called on Aunt Fanny on Pacific Avenue, it was fun. We would walk down to Pacific. There, Mother would wave to the motorman on the "dinky streetcar," which obligingly stopped for us in mid-block. I happily clutched the two nickels Mother had given me to pay the conductor for both of us. The streetcar had two attached cars, one outdoors, the other indoors. It lurched about so that it was hard to keep one's balance, and I would cling to Mother, giggling at the jiggling. The motorman clanged the bell repeatedly and loudly to amuse me, and I pushed at the door, pretending that my action speeded us on our way. The "dinky" was more like an amusement park mechanism than a practical transport. For such an occasion I would have to wear a hat, a wide-brimmed affair with streamers down the back and an uncomfortable elastic band under my chin so that it would not blow off.

Another afternoon Mother would accompany me to the orthodontist. For years I had a mouth filled with fitted gold bands that needed periodic adjustment. Mother would laugh and say to Aunt Alice, "No wonder Dr. Suggett drives a Rolls-Royce." I thought that the gold hardware clamped about my teeth was most distinguished and I neither saw the joke nor the connection with the Rolls. To get to the dentist, we took the cable car and sat outside, possibly to make the visit a pleasant adventure. This was fun for me, especially when the conductor called out lustily, "Hold your hats 'round the curve." We would take hold of a post with one hand and hang onto our hats with the other. As a special treat after the visit to the dentist, we walked to Maskey's Candies on Kearny Street and had an "all-around chocolate," the very finest ice-cream soda. This was indeed a dispensation in our family, inasmuch as anything eaten between meals was thought to spoil one's appetite.

Mother, Aunt Alice, my sister, and cousins, would sometimes troop down to Sommer and Kaufman's to buy shoes. The type of shoe is indicative of the times. The shoes selected were either "school shoes," which were Spaulding's brown-and-white oxfords with crepe soles, or "party shoes"—shiny black patent-leather Mary Janes with a bow on the toe and a strap across the instep. Needless to say, shoes should provide what the sisters termed "firm support."

When my mother visited school in order to confer with my teacher, I was always proud and happy to see her. Her presence seemed to warm the classroom and give me a special feeling of security. During those days, she was the president of the Parent-Teacher Association. Her self-conscious dread of addressing an audience led her to practicing public speaking in front of Aunt Alice. "Now don't make me laugh; this must be serious," she was often heard to say by way of prelude.

Mrs. Kissenmachel came to our house once a week. She was the sewing lady who mended, altered, and turned hems, cuffs, and collars up, about, and all around for Aunt Alice and Mother. I liked visiting her up in the attic sewing room adjacent to our playroom. I would watch her agile feet pedal the sewing machine with rapid fury and admire the way she snipped and snapped threads between her teeth. Quite suddenly, Mrs. Kissenmachel became Mrs. Rolphs. This was puzzling to me, but I understood it had to do with anti-German feelings after the First World War. It offended me when grown-ups laughed as I explained, "Mrs. Kissenmachel is Mrs. Rolphs because of the Germans." (For the same reason, my family name was changed from *Brandenstein*.) Another day brought belligerent Miss Elling, who stormed through the rooms like a trooper. She came equipped with broom, duster, pails, and a machine that roared around routing clouds of dust from obscure corners. Miss Elling wore a bandanna tied around her head and big white gloves over her hands. She made everything smell of strong ammonia. I had to be up and about and out of her way. She turned everything topsy-turvy, including my favorite books. *Black Beauty, The Wizard of Oz, The Water Babies*—all were dumped in disorder on the floor. When no one came to the house to scour, scrub, stitch, sew, and disturb the cherished *organized* disorder of my books, dolls, and toys, other industrious individuals occupied the time with polishing up my dormant skills and mending what Mother thought were gaps in an ordinary school day's education. Both Alice and Florine subscribed to Victorian standards as to what comprised a proper education. As a consequence, all of us took private lessons after school hours and on Saturday mornings.

One afternoon a week, we had horseback riding. I felt awkward wearing my riding habit to public school, attired in breeches and leggings, fitted jacket, a necktie, and a little velveteen jockey cap. The other children made fun of my costume, but there was no way out of it. Mother was oblivious to differences in backgrounds and values. She seemed to think that everyone lived in her kind of world, a sheltered one of means, maids, and lessons. The lame old French riding master, Captain Dillon, overawed me as he shouted imperiously in French from a ringside seat and pounded his cane by way of accent: *"Trot, bébé, trot!"* Or, *"Petit galop, bébé. Alors, galop, bébé!"* My heart lurched at this command, for I was frightened of the towering horse who snorted through flaring nostrils and pawed the ground impatiently. The English saddle seemed dangerously slippery to me, and I continually fumbled due to my temptation to hang onto the horse's mane for security. I struggled to do as instructed, but it was far easier to ride informally, Western style, as we did at summer resorts when we accompanied my parents on open trails. There I could cling to the pommel of a Mexican saddle with no one to correct or direct me —devoid of the monotony of riding around in the ring. I wondered at my mother easily riding astride some old country nag, for she told me that she had learned to ride sidesaddle, wearing long flowing skirts in the manner of her day.

There came a time when Mother and Aunt Alice thought it would be a great benefit to their small daughters to take what was termed interpretive dancing from a certain Mrs. Rush. I assume this was to develop imagination, grace, poise, mobility, and a sense of rhythm and music. I do not know how Alice and Florine stumbled upon this theory, nor how they discovered Mrs. Rush. A half century later, I still wonder if Mrs. Rush ever succeeded in promoting any of these qualities in anyone. The lessons took place in my great-aunt Carrie's attic. Aunt Carrie, who was one of my grandmother's sisters, lived in a large neighboring Franklin Street house. Her granddaughters were enrolled in the class along with us. We wore nothing but chiffon shifts, to allow complete freedom of movement, and went barefoot on the cold hardwood floor. Mrs. Rush instructed us to close our eyes, relax, and drift into a receptive mood of listening as music played on a squeaking Victrola. We were told to move with the music into any sort of floating dance we felt it inspired. I know very well what it inspired in me: uncontrollable giggling. With eyes closed and arms waving, I always bumped into the other girls. This, of course, ruined the effect of drifting melodiously and threw my sister and me into spasms of laughter, thus disrupting the class. Finally Mrs. Rush suggested that my sister and I take a few private lessons, hoping that we might exert self-control when we were by ourselves. This did not work, either. We continued to giggle and bump. Interpretative dancing was dropped from our curriculum.

Another afternoon we attended Miss Miller's dancing class. I rushed home from school to change into my Mary Jane patent slippers and a Mrs. Siem party dress, and ran off to dancing class. Perspiring boys with damp hands clutched me around the waist nervously as we tried to follow one another. Keeping time with the beat of the piano and Miss Miller's sharp calls, "One, two, and a-one-two-three," we moved back and forth, forth and back, gasping and grasping. Between dances, the girls lined up, seated on a long, hard side bench, wondering in agony if there would be a next partner. The boys clustered together, snickering at the door, anxious to get away, and on occasions one or two did just that: they simply bolted.

On Saturday mornings, when there was no school, we had still more lessons. A Madame Bigone, the French teacher, came at eight. Miss Levy, the piano teacher, came at nine. Those two ladies were kept busy shuffling up and down Franklin Street, instructing Alice's and Florine's children. Such cultural accomplishments were considered necessary by the sisters; it was their *duty* to expose their children to learning, whether it took or not. Aunt Alice and Mother spoke both French and German fluently, and Mother played four-handed piano with my brother or a friend of hers until her fingers were too stiff to continue.

The ritual of Saturday lessons accomplished, we were free to glide up and down Franklin Street on roller skates and to play boisterously with the neighboring children. Often we boarded a streetcar under a maid's supervision and went to the Woman's Athletic Club on Sutter Street for swimming lessons. My cousins and sister seemed to enjoy the steamy locker room and the salty swimming pool far more than I. I took refuge in pretending enthusiasm because I did not want to be different. At times I convinced myself that it was fun, but on the whole I disliked the itchy black wool suits with W.A.C. emblazoned on them, and I resented having my long hair pulled up under a protective shammy (*chamois*) and wearing the tight rubber cap that went over it. I felt as if my head would burst from these bindings. Despite the layers of protective paraphernalia, my hair was damp when swimming was over. We were not allowed to leave the club until our hair was bone-dry, for there was always the menace of catching grippe, and so we would spend tedious sessions under a monstrous hair dryer. The hood of the dryer seemed to suck life and breath away with a roaring, hot wind.

There was sometimes a Saturday luncheon party at another girl's house or at home—or better yet, in the muffled elegance of the Club's dining room, where one could order for oneself and feel grown-up. On special Saturdays Mother and Aunt Alice gathered the clan to lunch in the gilt and stained glass of the Palace Hotel's Garden Court. Mother recalled her wedding night in the Palace in 1902 and earlier days when carriages drove into the very courtyard where we were lunching. The court, with its vast cathedral heights, had an aura of the romantic past. I can still taste the famous Garden Court Salad, luscious white cubes of chicken stacked on an enormous fresh artichoke heart. Another Saturday we might meet under the famous landmark clock at the St. Francis Hotel, lunch in the Mural Room, and proceed to the Orpheum Theater's vaudeville. Here performed an acrobat who walked on his hands with as equal ease as on his feet. My cousin Liz and I practiced this walking upside down for many months, thinking how delightful it would be to astonish the family and enter the dining room in like manner at Sunday dinner. We never quite mastered it. Or, after lunch, we might attend a newly invented "talkie" film down on Market Street. We enjoyed sobbing through sound movies, such

as *Wings*, and Al Jolson in *The Singing Fool*. Those few Saturday afternoons we were indulgently allowed to spend at Playland, out at the
beach, were almost too exciting to endure. "Shoot-the-Chutes" and
the "Big Dipper" churned and turned my stomach. To ride up to pre-
cipitous heights and rush down at a perpendicular angle smothered
me with heart-stopping fright. It was a punishment to be endured in
the name of fun. To my dismay, this was consented to, provided we
didn't "gorge on greasy hotdogs and sticky pink cotton candy."

Special treats were current musical comedies and operettas. The
lilt of melodies, the emoting in sound: those lyric duets of lovers har-
monizing from melding hearts, and waltzing in perfect unison, these
are indelible moments of my earliest theater memories. Those handsome leading men: the Red Shadow from *The Desert Song, The Student
Prince, The Chocolate Soldier, The Merry Widow*'s ardent suitors—these
were the favorite heroes of my romantic world of dreams in which
I was the beautiful leading lady. Aunt Alice and Mother thought the
legitimate theater was a form of art, but movies were, to them, "sensa-
tional trash." We adamantly insisted that we enjoyed sorrowing over
our fictional shadows, emerging from the movies with sodden handkerchiefs and reddened eyes. Mother and Aunt Alice were permissive, and ever eager for us to have a good time, so we continued our
movie adventures sporadically. Exposing the children to culture was
important to the sisters. As a result, I found myself attending several
matinées at André Férrier's French Theatre, which was designed for
the entertainment of San Francisco's French community. I strained to
applaud with the rest of the audience and managed to summon a few
polite and hollow laughs while others guffawed in appreciation. I had
no command of French; I was lost in blank incomprehension. It was
quite a relief when the final curtain fell.

For several years I was persuaded to attend Temple Emanu-El

Sunday school with my older siblings and cousins. When they were confirmed, I stopped going, too. We thought it was important what we wore to Sunday classes, and we especially wished to look very grown-up. Our parents believed exercise was essential. So, dressed in our best, with contraband pomade and compacts hidden in our bags, we walked in a group to Emanu-El, swinging our arms industriously. This, even when Emanu-El moved far out to Arguello and Lake from the dowtown location on Sutter near Powell.

On a Sunday afternoon, we might elect to go to the band concert at the Music Stand in Golden Gate Park. As a child, I gathered fallen leaves and discarded programs that littered the ground and, pretending that I was an usher, distributed the programs and leaves to the audience. After the concert, we would stop at the Japanese Tea Garden, sip green tea, admire the kimono-clad waitresses tripping about daintily on their sandaled feet, clamber over the steep, high bridge, and carefully fold away our souvenirs—tissue-thin paper napkins with delicate watercolor scenes scrolled on them, and Japanese flags that were folded inside the napkins. It was fun to hold the flags out of the automobile window and let them flap in the wind.

Usually the sisters were home with their families in the evenings. The pace was quiet at night. Entertaining did not include cocktail parties. There might be a dinner party, a symphony, or an opera to attend. The sisters particularly enjoyed going to the theater, including the local offerings of the Henry Duffey players at the Alcazar on O'Farrell Street, or the visiting reviews at the Orpheum, featuring entertainers such as Al Jolson, Eddie Cantor, and Ed Wynn. They also liked recitations such as Bob Mantel declaiming Shakespeare. Aunt Alice and Uncle Sam were devotees of Gilbert and Sullivan operettas. When the D'Oyly Carte Company performed in San Francisco, the family enthusiastically attended all the shows and hummed the catchy melodies for days. We attended other spectacles and performances. From Germany came Max Reinhardt, who produced and directed *The Miracle,* a drama so vast in scale that it was staged at the Civic Auditorium. The actors rushing up and down the aisles, chains rattling, and other effects of Reinhardt's concept frightened more than thrilled me.

We heard Yehudi Menuhin, who played the violin with the depth of a mature genius in his Lord Fauntleroy suit and gold curls. Menuhin was my contemporary, and I wished I, too, were a child prodigy—he made it look so easy.

The evenings that were given over to dinner parties were dress-up affairs. Father wore a tuxedo, and Mother wore sequined velvet or chiffon with matching slippers. Mother's beauty preparations consisted of rubbing her cheeks with terry cloth so that they would turn pink, and biting her lips to redden them. She would wear a frown plaster to bed the night before the party in order to erase her forehead lines. "Oh, ding it," or "Oh, shoot," she would mutter as she guiltily and surreptitiously dusted a bit of talcum powder across her nose. No powder on Aunt Alice's face was ever seen, not ever. All her life, her face looked as if it had been polished to a magical burnish. She always appeared scrubbed and radiant. Her face had as much sheen as her twinkling dark eyes. She breezed a special aroma, an indescribably clean, sweet fragrance of soap and water lathered. It was far more seductive than French perfume. Many courses were served at formal dinner functions, each accompanied by a different wine chosen from the cellar's chilly, double-locked storeroom. There the various bottles were laid out, categorized, and labeled in specially built niches, like babies in cradles. Although Father enjoyed selecting his wines, he balked at the tedious dinners where plate succeeded plate and numerous bores toasted and made speeches; then he felt trapped. Father was of a restless nature and would have preferred today's short-order counters to yesterday's prolonged meals. I remember a time when the clock struck eleven. Father felt that it was bedtime and disappeared. Shortly afterwards, dressed in his bathrobe, he called from the top of the stairs, "Florine, come up to bed. It's late." I'm not sure who was more mortified, the lingering guests or Mother. Uncle Sam was more diplomatic. If he tired of sitting at the dining table for prolonged periods of time, he inquired caustically, "Any more meat courses? If not, we can get up." I found the approach hilariously funny no matter how often he repeated it, for meat would have been ridiculous after mountains of flaming baked Alaska or puffed soufflés had been served.

I liked the bustle and excitement that preceded formal dinners. All day long the doorbell rang: the iceman delivered blocks of ice; young Sal Sancimino from Swan Oyster Depot delivered Blue Point oysters; the Campagna brothers delivered a brace of pheasants or ducks or quail; and the florist, Albert Stein, came laden with multicolored bouquets. Sometimes I watched Wah crank the heavy ice-cream machine out in the back garden. And sometimes I helped the cook shell bushels of green peas, savoring their sweetness as I wrestled them from their pods. I loved seeing Mother and Aunt Alice gussied up. They carried either beaded or petit-point bags, whose sole contents included either a single monogrammed handkerchief or a folding, diamond-studded lorgnette. On occasion they wore long white kid gloves with multitudes of tiny buttons. The glove-hands generally dangled from a slit in the wrist, freeing the women's hands, so that the gloves were ornamental rather than practical.

When guests arrived I was banished upstairs, where I could eavesdrop from the first landing. My head hung over the banister, but I would withdraw it quickly if someone looked up. I'd listen to the polite murmur of voices as they cried, "Good evening, my dear, how well you are looking, and have you heard the latest about Sadie and Albert?" I'd hear the sliding doors to the dining room open and the exclamations of delight as the guests entered by couples to seek their seats. Sometimes I got dressed up just to go downstairs for a few minutes to curtsy and say, "How do you do?" to the guests. Barely glancing at me, a guest might murmur, "My, how you've grown, child! We'll have to put a brick on your head!"

The quiet evenings my parents spent at home gave me a feeling of comforting security. Dinner was served promptly at seven. Tardiness evoked a severe reprimand. Menus were fairly predictable. On Wednesday we had my favorite meal. It was the cook's afternoon off, and she would have prepared a roast capon in advance so that the maid could heat it easily and serve it with baked potatoes. On Friday we had fish out of respect to the Catholic waitresses. Even when there was no Catholic in the house, however, Friday was forever the absolute fixed fish day. The fish had to be freshly caught that morning from San Francisco shores. When a leg of lamb was served, Father would give me the gristled chops off the end. If we had roast beef, he gave me a thick pink slice away from the heel. Along with my portion of beef, he thought it very funny to place a large bouquet of decorative parsley on my plate. "It's good for you," he would chuckle. Father was surely a pioneer of today's health faddists. Butter had to be imbedded in ice, impossible to spread. Crackers had to be like hardtack to benefit one's teeth. Cake had to be stale for good digestion. Once my brothers, sister, and I put dog biscuits on his butter plate, but he did not think it was funny. When the cake platter came in, Father eyed it warily, tested it with a cake knife, and asked when it had been baked. Desserts were often bowls of sago, bread, or rice pudding. Mother urged me to eat these globulous concoctions, which tasted like glue to me. "Delicious! It tastes just like ice cream," Mother chanted. I knew bread pudding was her method of using stale bread, and rice pudding was served because rice was one of Father's businesses. Sago and tapioca Father thought good for one. We preferred fruit compotes, applesauce, fresh-juice gelatins, and any cake that was not from Father's stale supply. Father thought it healthiest to snatch a fresh apple from the centerpiece of fruits. "Something to sink one's teeth into." He would cut the apple in half and inelegantly place the other half back in the bowl, causing Mother to say, "Wait and see what dessert is, Ed, that's not a good example for the children. Who do you think will eat the other half?" I promptly volunteered. I knew it would be a good apple; if it wasn't, Father discarded it immediately and cut another.

After dinner, Mother and Father filed up to the back sitting room. Often the gas log was lit in the fireplace. The room was warm, cozy; it seemed filled with love and closeness. I sensed that Aunt Alice and Uncle Sam had gone to their own front upstairs sitting room and that my cousins were feeling the same protective warmth. Settled under a reading lamp, Mother might phone her sister for the tenth time that day, or she might help my sister or me with homework. She had faultless knowledge of arithmetic and spelling, due to her education in Miss Murison's strict young-women's seminary. If she were doing needlepoint, she might be heard to sigh, "Oh, dear me, and my dear, too!" or if the work was difficult, quite vehemently, for a mild lady, "I could jump out of my skin!" The great cursing phrase was, "Oh, ding it!" From time to time she played Russian Bank or Casino with Father. I do not recall seeing her read, although Father was an avid reader. I think Mother considered reading a waste of time, even though she guided me to good literature. She was forever dedicated to accomplishing something, and she liked the results to show.

On those occasions when my Aunt Alice and mother exchanged dinners, they would walk from one house to the other, marching up and down Franklin Street regardless of weather. Frequently my parents had additional, informal guests: widowed sisters, stray uncles, a visiting cousin. The house would darken and quiet down at 10:00 p.m., with a ritual of good-night hugs, and Father bolting the front door and adjusting the grandfather clock on the landing.

Top left: Alice and Frances Bransten, photographed in 1922 at ages twelve and eight. Bottom left: Grandfather clock in the foyer at 2007 Franklin Street, 1972. Top right: Samuel Lilienthal and Alice Haas's engagement portrait, circa 1909. Middle right: Florine and Edward Brandenstein (changed to Bransten during World War I), with sons Edward and William. Bottom right: The kitchen at 2007 Franklin Street, 1972, including "state-of-the-art" 1927 gas stovetop and oven.

Top left: Alice Haas Lilienthal in Atherton in 1936 with Stephan Moses. **Top right:** Garden Court, Palace Hotel, after 1906. A favorite destination for Alice and Florine following downtown shopping trips or on special Saturdays. Photo courtesy of San Francisco History Center, San Francisco Public Library. **Middle right:** Chutes at the Beach, 1930. Photo courtesy of Western Neighborhoods Project/OpenSFHistory.org. **Bottom left:** Portrait of laundryman employed by the Branstens ("Wah") taken at the Hen Yin Gock gallery in Chinatown. Date unknown. **Bottom right:** Japanese Tea Garden, Golden Gate Park, 1935. Alice and Florine would take the children for green tea and fortune cookies following Sunday concerts at the Music Stand. Photo courtesy of Western Neighborhoods Project/OpenSFHistory.org.

Betrothals and Romances

◇◇

Mother and Aunt Alice were born romantics. They loved talking and hearing about love and enthused over lovelorn dramas and sentimental plays. They whispered, surmised, and giggled over possible espousals with heart, soul, fuss, and fanfare, and enjoyed feting new couples. The Sunday after my brother Edward announced his engagement to Cathryn, he found his chair was bound to Cathryn's with a silken white cord at the dinner table. On top of the two chairs roped closely together was a large white satin bow interlaced with orange blossoms. It was a bit embarrassing for a young man to sit under these flowers and bows, but such was the spirit of his doting mother and aunt.

At nineteen Liz was the first of us to have love enter her life. When Liz's romance began, we cousins followed it avidly and were as infatuated with Jim as if we were the objects of his courtship. Jim had attended Cambridge University before coming to live in San Francisco from his home in London. His English polish swept us off our feet, and I, for one, could not understand why Liz seemed to have *her* feet on the ground. At eighteen I was as romantic as my mother. I swooned and dreamed vicariously and did not understand what there was to wait for or think over. Liz's romance progressed that year as Jim trailed her to Tahoe Tavern, to the Atherton summer home, to Stanford University, and to Franklin Street. At last, Liz said yes on a summer's day in Atherton. Jim attempted to ask Aunt Alice for a mother's consent. After those many months of prelude, Aunt Alice was surely aware of Jim's wishes as he pursued her through the gardens. She walked rapidly, busily sorting and picking flowers, seemingly preoccupied with the task at hand. She was deeply fond of Jim, but facing up to this conversation so embarrassed her that she hid behind her gloves, shears, and flowers. She turned on Jim abruptly. "I have no time to chat now, Jim. Don't you know this is my flower day? On Fridays I pick and arrange the flowers." Obviously, he finally caught up with her, for the engagement was announced. Mother was as excited as her sister. She rushed to the guest room where Jim was installed and knocked on the door. "Don't come in," Jim called out. "I'm in the shower." "Oh, that's all right, dearie," Mother called back. "It's *only* Aunt Florine!" Jim has never forgotten this introduction to his new aunt. When Mother saw Liz and Jim together, the first thing she demanded of the shy young lovers was, "Now, let me see you kiss."

Liz and Jim's wedding in September 1934 was an Aunt Alice masterpiece. The ceremony took place under a wisteria arbor in the flower-filled Atherton gardens. Liz, diminutive next to her tall bridegroom, glowed in a classic white gown replete with delicate lace and a full sweeping train. The color scheme was Alice's favorite—royal blue and emerald green. The six bridesmaids and maid of honor wore long green taffeta off-the-shoulder dresses and carried bouquets of blue-green water lilies. I was a bridesmaid, but I got so excited walking down the gravel path that served as the aisle that I veered off in the wrong direction. Over three hundred guests sat down to a champagne luncheon served at tables surrounding the swimming pool.

That day the pool appeared to be a Monet-like green lagoon. We were in a blue-green world of romance and beauty. We danced on a canvas floor laid over the tennis court, a flower-strewn awning above us for protection from the noonday sun. As Liz and Jim left for their honeymoon, it seemed as if the wedding were the happy end to a fairy tale enhanced by Aunt Alice's magic wizardry.

My own romance began in 1937 when I attended Barnard College in New York City. I was introduced to Hans Rothmann at a dinner party given by mutual friends named Raiss. Hans had fled Hitler's Germany from his native Berlin, where he had studied medicine. I was thrilled with our courtship but still had to complete my senior year. Hans was instrumental in my passing a difficult astronomy class, required for graduation. He presented me with an antique astronomy print of a comet that I showed my instructor—and then I passed the course! Hans later inscribed the print "to the astronomical girl." I had fallen in love with Hans, but was unsure about getting married right away as I wanted to secure a job. During Christmas of 1937 I fled Hans and New York for San Francisco to think over Hans's proposal of marriage. On December 31st, Hans flew out to San Francisco to meet my parents, to keep a New Year's Eve date with me, and to press his courtship. He telegraphed his arrival time while still en route, so that they felt besieged and unprepared. The morning Hans arrived, he telephoned that he was at the Fairmont Hotel. I called for him on foot, and we walked the many blocks home to Franklin Street for the introductions. Years later, Hans asked me why we had walked. An interesting question. Walking had been so ingrained in me that I had not considered an alternative. Mother waited for us attired in her Hoover apron. Our Christmas tree still stood in the parlor and the very second she met Hans, she untied a gift from the tree to give to him. The gift consisted of a piece of soap and one of Mother's hand-knitted washrags. Hans confessed later that he felt rather like a chastised child in need of these supplies.

In early February of 1938, Mother, Father, my sister, and I went to New York on the sleek 20th Century train. Mother, who had never had a drink in her life, accompanied me into the club car and choked down a cocktail in honor of my romance. In New York as in San Francisco, everything had to be properly conducted as to the correct time and place. A couple of days before the wedding, Hans and I went for a walk on the crowded streets of Manhattan. Hans took my hand in casual affection. Mother was aghast. "Oh, no, children. No one knows you're engaged. It hasn't been announced. You mustn't hold hands on the street, or everyone will know." I looked at the rush of passersby hurrying about their own affairs. I suggested to Mother that it was doubtful that anyone cared, but she did not see it that way. One didn't kiss or hold hands in public until one was properly betrothed. In fact, she formally addressed Hans as "Doctor" until after the wedding. In a few days' time, Mother made all the arrangements for my wedding at the Savoy Plaza Hotel. About a hundred guests came to attend the afternoon nuptials. It was traditional to the last detail. My sister, Alice, was a quavering maid of honor in rose *peau de soie*. My cousin Billy Haas came from Harvard to be best man. Rabbi Louis Newman performed the ceremony. The altar was banked with white flowers, arranged by Mother. There was music, dancing, champagne, hors d'oeuvres. Thousands of miles from home, Mother had contrived, staged, and managed the whole affair with miraculous, creative energy. Hans and I sailed for Bermuda on a ten-day honeymoon while my parents remained in New York awaiting our return. Mother had bought me an exquisitely fragile, expensive trousseau nightgown. She met us at the ship when it docked and asked if I had enjoyed wearing the gown. I confessed that it had ripped on our wedding night. Mother insisted on wrapping it up and taking it back to San Francisco, where she indignantly returned it to I. Magnin's and actually received credit! Mother's naive persistence had won the day.

1938 was a year in which Mother was bombarded with the romances of three of her four children. During the summer of 1937, my two brothers vacationed together in Sun Valley. There they met a New York family, a mother, father, and their two daughters. The younger, Sue, was a Smith College senior. Brother William was smitten with Sue. The summer ended and they parted, but all that year they corresponded; and then William flew East to pursue his love. Sue wished to finish college before committing herself, and so William arranged to meet her and her parents in Jasper National Park the following summer. There the romance flourished and a wedding was planned for the following November in New York. The first thing William did was to telephone Mother and Father. Sue, at twenty-one, was modest and unassuming. She was awed and excited by the great ado that centered on her and William. William asked Sue to talk to Mother, but Sue was terrified at the thought of conversing with her future mother-in-law. What should she say, and how was she to express herself? She bravely pulled herself together, assuming her most courteous manner. Over the wires, from Alberta, Canada, to California, Sue's voice quaked, "How do you do, Mrs. Bransten? This is Sue." Mother's reply came without hesitation. "Hello, Sue darling. Tell me, darling, does your father like chocolate pudding?" Mother's mind was on the dinner she was planning to serve when they all arrived in San Francisco so that they could meet and get to know each other. She was thrilled by the romance, and never dreamed of questioning William's judgment. Sue, somewhat bewildered by Mother's question, never felt ill at ease with her again. There was that down-to-earth, natural simplicity and directness about Mother that made everyone comfortable.

When Mother and Aunt Alice expected grandchildren, they immediately began to knit a particular style of blanket whose intricate pattern had been handed down to them from their mother's maid-companion, Martha. The wool was white, with sprigs of pink rosebuds and green leaves. As soon as anyone saw the sisters busy with their blankets, it heralded the coming of a baby as surely as if all the trumpets in heaven were blaring lullabies. I believe the sisters cast stitches on their needles the very moment of conception. At the beginning of a pregnancy, when only the grandmother had been told, and someone hinted suspicion, Mother and Aunt Alice would duck and blush into their knitting, purse their lips, shake their heads, explode in guilty giggles, and hush each other with nudges. Their coy performance told the tale far better than any verbal confirmation. The second signal they gave was to trim the bassinet in which every newborn in the family had slept since the turn of the century. Their painstaking efforts required months of stitching and care before it was considered ready. When my daughter Susan was born, the white wicker rocking cradle was carefully shipped to New York. Pink and blue ribbons were woven through its wicker slots, while an overhead organdy canopy, interlined with pink silk, was suspended, falling gracefully around the body of the bassinet. On the very top rested a pink-and-blue satin bow, its streamers mingling in the cascading organdy curtain. When Susan graduated to a crib, the cradle was shipped back to San Francisco. Billy, the son I bore fourteen months later, did not share in this family tradition, as other new mothers in the family had prior claim.

John, my younger son, was born in San Francisco while my mother was out of town. He chose the inconsiderate hour of seven in the evening. The obstetrician, Dr. Zach Coblentz, rushed to the hospital from a dinner party and my Aunt Alice arrived with equal speed, carrying a sandwich for the doctor, so concerned was she that he might miss a meal.

The cycle of love-marriage-baby-carriage rejuvenated and delighted Aunt Alice and Mother. They were deeply loved and appreciated as mothers and mothers-in-law, and they performed their grandmother and great-aunt roles like fairy godmothers.

Top left: Wedding Portrait of Alice and Samuel Lilienthal, November 3, 1909, in the rear garden of 2007 Franklin Street. Three more family members wore that dress. **Top right:** Wedding portrait of Hans and Frances Rothmann, February 11, 1938. **Bottom:** Wedding of Elizabeth Lilienthal Gerstley, September 7, 1934. Left to right: Ann Lilienthal (Haber), Marjorie Gunst (Stern), Ann Rosener (Perls), Suzanna Ward, Elizabeth Lilienthal Gerstley, Madeleine Haas (Russell), Frances Lilienthal (Stein), Margaret Samuels (Frank), Frances Bransten (Rothmann). At the wisteria arbor in the Atherton garden.

Top: Loving banter between Hans Rothmann and Frances, his "astronomical girl," late 1930s. **Middle left:** Nearly forty years after Alice wed Samuel at 2007 Franklin Street, they hosted the marriage of their niece Madeleine Haas to Léon Russell in 1946. Left to right: Alice, Madeleine, and Léon receive guests as they arrive. **Bottom left:** Madeleine Haas on her wedding day. **Bottom right:** Florine's Wedding: Alice Haas, Florine Haas Brandenstein (later Bransten), Florence Hellman (Ehrman), 1903.

THE PARTY GIVERS

My husband had his first encounter with my mother and aunt's party-giving ways when we were first married and Mother visited us in New York. She loaded Hans down with seventy individually gift-wrapped silver dollars, which he was to please take to her Uncle Louis Greene, who was stopping in a New York hotel while celebrating his seventieth birthday. Hans obliged and managed to stagger to the hotel and deliver the elaborately packaged gifts to Mother's quite affluent uncle.

The sisters were dedicated to finding causes for parties. Thus we had a party to acknowledge Prohibition and another to acknowledge the Depression, one to tidy their homes by distributing possessions and others to honor certain milestone ages. Often there were parties just to have a party, and an imaginative celebration would have to be dreamed up. During Prohibition a so-called Meat-Market Party was staged at the Victorian house on Franklin Street. The meat market, appropriately decked out with sawdust floor and haunches of steer hanging from hooks, was made up as a setting to conceal a bootlegging front. Uncle Charlie composed a libretto to the tune of "Tea for Two," which he sang to Mother's accompaniment on the piano.

There were many wonderful parties held in the gardens of Atherton. Once the sisters collaborated to give Liz, Madeleine, and me a circus party. Our photographs were superimposed on posters that hung around the tennis court, where we danced. There was I, swinging on a trapeze, Liz walking a tightrope, and Madeleine in a ballet skirt straddling a hoop. A guest, Edgar Kahn, obligingly assumed the role of strongman and performed various feats, including the flexing of his muscles. Daguerreotypes were taken, snow cones and pink popcorn served, and there were funhouse mirrors everywhere, where one could gape at a distorted reflection.

My sixteenth-birthday party remains a landmark in my memory. A Swedish lady, whom we fondly called Mama Gravanda, had a large house on Pacific Avenue. There she served smorgasbord to select clients, took in young single boarders, taught weaving, and both instructed and held Swedish folk dancing evenings. I delighted in her buffets and I loved wandering through the rooms, examining the looms and patterns woven by her students. I especially enjoyed her group of young boarders and the swinging in and out and about to the rhythmic melodies of the folk dancing. Mama Gravanda was a joyful hostess, always dressed in a Swedish-peasant costume, clapping her hands for food or dance, and beaming smiles from her ruddy, round face. I requested that my birthday dinner be held in these picturesque surroundings of a miniature Sweden. Mother stealthily secured a baby photo of every guest I intended to invite and had the original idea of transferring duplicates of these photos onto the place cards. Everyone had to find his seat by recognizing himself as a baby. Embarrassed squeals of delight, surprise, and tickled egos filled the house upon discovery. After the hearty buffet we danced exuberantly while Mama Gravanda shouted instructions, stamping and clapping to the boisterous beat of the music.

My sister Alice's eighteenth birthday fell in 1928, the year that marked the grande finale to the roaring twenties. It was a period when hostesses in our circle vied with each other in giving elaborate costume balls. I remember my brother Ed dressed as a Venetian gondolier, and wondered how he would manage on the dance floor with the long boatman's oar he carried. I marveled at the descriptions my brothers gave of the parties they attended. The debutante of the evening might float into the room on some elaborate contraption. Perhaps she would arrive sitting on top of a papier-mâché birthday cake or make her appearance stepping out of a seashell! Mother, never to be outdone, conceived of holding a fiesta for my sister Alice. During a summer in Santa Barbara, Mother was enchanted by the annual Spanish fête and so on November 16, 1928, at eight o'clock in the evening, the Colonial and the Italian rooms of the St. Francis Hotel were transformed into a romantic Spanish town for five hundred guests. Both a Spanish and an American orchestra played. A couple tangoed on a raised platform and postured gracefully to the accompaniment of their castanets. The rooms were filled with caballeros and their señoritas; all the guests wore Spanish costumes. Twirling their sombreros and whirling full, sparkling skirts, they flung themselves into the Charleston and the foxtrot.

Madeleine, Liz, and I, the youngest at the party, were assigned the role of cigarette girls to keep us occupied. We had a fine excuse to stop at each table, proffer our wares, and observe the diners in their fancy costumes. I loved my lettuce-green organdy dress trimmed with pink roses. A grown man of eighteen deigned to dance with me. I was fourteen years old, but to this day I appreciate the courtly attention Lad Hellman bestowed on me that evening. During dinner, broccoli was served. I had never seen it before. I was told that it had just been invented—the result of crossing cauliflower with asparagus, and found it intriguing. Mother decorated each of the sixty-odd tables herself and seated each guest with studied planning. She wore herself out, trusting to no one in her quest for perfection. As a result, following the party Mother underwent a rest cure of several months' duration. That was the last of such elaborate affairs.

In the midst of the Depression, Aunt Alice and Uncle Sam gave a "Hard Times" party in Atherton for their children. Each guest received an authentic-looking book of coupons containing three tickets: one for dancing, one for dining, and one for drinks. As a concession to frugality, hamburgers and hotdogs, replacing squab or filet, were served from booths.

Mother and Aunt Alice were as creative in preparing us to go to parties we were invited to as they were to those they hosted. Alice's son, Ernest, was of an age whereby he usually found himself escorting three bashful maidens to a dance—Liz, Madeleine, and me. We never seemed to find anyone who wished to take us, or with whom we wished to go to a party, other than our comfortable, reliable, and handsome member of the family, Ernest. Once when we were invited to a costume party, Ernest dressed as a sheik and we dressed suitably to represent his harem. What a hilarious outing it was to go with Aunt Alice to Goldstein's Costume Rentals on Market Street to choose our costumes! I selected a lavender sari; Madeleine, turquoise, and Liz, canary yellow. We added multitudes of jangling anklets and bracelets out of Goldstein's jewel-crammed drawers. Ernest turned into a magnificent sheik in bright-green pantaloons and a purple turban, complete with tassel. We giggled hysterically throughout our fittings. Aunt Alice turned to a bewildered Mr. Goldstein in despair. "I don't know what to do with these children, dearie. Aren't they the silly ones?" Her apology threw us into further fits of uncontrollable giggles.

When the sisters were older and their children married, they decided to tidy their houses and simultaneously give pleasure by distributing some of the possessions they had collected through the years. One day we received an invitation: "Extra, Extra—Read All About It. An auction to take place at 1735 Franklin Street, on Sunday Evening, after dinner. Only Chocolate Dollars Accepted." Once, many years earlier, the sisters cleaned house. They sold several objects to a dealer, but then reconsidered. Each, unknown to the other, rushed out to Mr. Goldenberg, the dealer, to buy back the other's things, at a higher price. Out of consideration for one another, neither wanted the other to be deprived.

The Sunday evening of Mother's auction, her living room was set up for the event with all the proper accoutrements. On her old oak clothes tree hung a plumed gay-nineties hat, a lace-trimmed gray silk gown indented with a minute Victorian waistline and a flowing "bertha" collar, a gentleman's bowler hat, and silver-handled cane. Beneath the clothes tree were cracked high shoes covered with yellow spats and a tiny pair of shriveled ladies' boots with their laces broken. Stacked on card tables were tarnished consommé cups, assorted Meissen and Limoges demitasses, an old magic lantern with stacks of slides, a couple of intricately beaded handbags, a silvered reticule, an ivory shoehorn, an oriental bud vase, lacquered boxes, a pile of ancient phonograph records, sheet music, and other oddities.

Mother presented each couple with a box of Simon Brothers' chocolate dollars and rapped her gavel for attention. We had a riotous evening of confused bidding, often interrupted by the sounds we made as we munched our money. We swaggered home like pirates weighted down with booty.

One summer, a hilarious party took place in Atherton to fete visiting friends from London, the Lessers, who liked to gamble. Aunt

Alice arranged a room to resemble a casino and covered a table with green felt, stacking it high with chips. She walked about shaking a pair of dice to lend conviction to the scene, but she resembled a gracious hostess more than a tough croupier. Mother knew little about cards and nothing about poker, but she wanted to learn and join in a game. The rules were written down for her and she kept them carefully so that she might refer to them as she played. In the middle of dealing, however, she was called to the telephone. The interruption proved to be an irresistible opportunity for Jim and his friend Fred to arrange her hand so that she held a royal flush. Mother returned to the table, picked up her cards, stared at them and then at the rules, gasped in embarrassment, and could not keep an appropriate poker face. The stakes were infinitesimal, but she won what she felt were huge amounts from everyone. She apologized profusely, incapable of understanding her luck. The very next morning, Mother, wishing to compensate for her vast good fortune, rushed out to buy the losers an expensive gift, overwhelming them with surprise presents. Mother eventually discovered the "frame-up" and felt gratified by her "revenge."

Mother and Aunt Alice were far more adept at giving than receiving. Compliments were more difficult to give Mother and Aunt Alice than parties. They felt unworthy and shook their heads in deprecation, denying and rejecting any word of praise. Although they recognized virtues in others, they could not see anything special in themselves and would answer to applause with an embarrassed laugh. "Oh, don't be so silly; it's not true!" The giving of gifts was most difficult of all to accomplish. Instead of thanking us, they chided, "How can you be so extravagant," or "I don't deserve this at all. Now you take it right back, darling. I know you can use it. It's perfectly lovely, but..." The one birthday gift Mother enjoyed was a pair of silk stockings Father took out of her bureau drawer, which we then wrapped as new ones. Each year she enjoyed our jest and entered into the act by enthusing over our wise selection of just the right size and color.

Parties, thoughtfulness, love, gifts—these the sisters gave in immeasurable quantities. They embroidered our lives and the lives of others with their verve, their originality, and their generosity.

Top left: Charles Haas, Walter Haas, and Samuel Lilienthal, early twentieth century. **Center left**: Yosemite Valley, December 1925, with Alice seated to the right of tree, wearing hat. **Bottom left**: Yosemite Valley, December 1925. **Top right**: Alice and brother Charles, circa 1905. **Bottom right**: Samuel and Alice Lilienthal with children Frances, Elizabeth (front center), and Ernest, at "Rampart" on Truckee River, circa 1925.

Top left: Samuel Lilienthal at Atherton, 1950s. **Bottom left:** Lunching poolside at Atherton, 1936. Left to right: Cousin Katherine Simon, Josephine (waitress), and Samuel Lilienthal. **Top right:** Samuel and Alice playing tennis at Atherton, 1939. **Center right:** Frances Lilienthal in Atherton rose garden, 1930. **Bottom right:** Alice at Atherton by pool, 1930s.

TRAVELS WITH THE SISTERS

Trips with my mother and Aunt Alice were high adventure. In early days, travel was invested with the excitement of packing trunks, taking ferries, and sleeping on Pullman trains. It entailed making long lists of necessities, rolls of tissue paper in which to neatly fold miscellaneous trappings, and special silk containers for underwear and handkerchiefs and gloves. It meant hatboxes, shoe bags, shoe trees, and jewelry cases. A bar of Fels-Naptha soap was packed with which to scrub hotel bureau drawers, and a white top sheet to cover "those dirty hotel blankets everyone else has used." There were reams of tickets for the railroad, for the boat, for baggage. The trunk stood upright in one's room for several days in advance, heightening the sense of anticipation. When the trunk was wheeled away by Railroad Express the day before departure, we knew with happy certainty that vacation was about to begin. Mother's room seemed naked without her trunk. The only sign of the impending journey was a fitted overnight bag complete with hand mirror, clothes brush, buttonhook, soap dish, and nail buffer—all of which were strapped securely in their proper niches. Mother's fittings were in heavy embossed silver, with her initials scrolled on them. I liked touching the raised ornamentation. It was easy to go obediently to bed early the night before, because it signified preparing for departure. Mother would say, "You need a good rest; tomorrow is a busy day."

For several years our summer destination was Lake Tahoe. Our journey began with a ferryboat ride across the bay. I would scamper to the upper deck with a brown bag full of doughnuts to nibble and toss to the shrieking gray gulls that swooped down in pursuit of the boat. At the Oakland Mole a long black train would be waiting and a grinning redcap would welcome us aboard. When the train pulled out in a cloud of steam, I rushed to the observation car where I sat out in the open, waving, observing, and choking on the dust and cinders, especially when the train rumbled through a tunnel. I begged to sleep in the upper berth, where I could close the heavy green curtains on my private domain and pretend I was a princess. The motion of the car, the sounds of clicking wheels and moaning whistles made me feel sleepy and secure. Breakfasting on the train was a special treat. Seated by the window in the dining car we were served by a beaming black waiter who brought piping-hot silver dishes covered with white linen napery. What bliss to bite into hot, buttery muffins while watching fields and streams flash by! In the old days the Tahoe train stopped at the small mountain town of Truckee at six in the morning. Here we left our Pullman and transferred to a narrow-gauge train to ascend the steep slope. Later, wide tracks were laid and the big train delivered us to the pier at Tahoe Tavern. Either route was splendidly scenic as we clickety-clacked along, viewing towering pines, rugged rocks, and the flowing Truckee River. When we went directly to the Tavern's pier, it was breathtaking to come upon the aqua lake nestled between snowcapped mountains and rugged cliffs. Sometimes we went to Tahoe via the overnight Sacramento riverboat *Delta Queen*, to the state capitol. It was adventurous churning up the river, and it served to break the motor trip. After disembarking in Sacramento, we transferred into the automobiles that had accompanied us on the river-boat. There were times when we drove the entire distance to Tahoe, often breaking the long journey by an overnight stay at the Senator Hotel in Sacramento, where it was always far too hot to sleep. Early the next morning we started out again. Bumping over the narrow, winding roads, we frequently had a flat tire or an overheated radiator, so that we were compelled to rest the overworked automobile. Long ago, the roundabout routes were difficult; we sweated as we chugged through the hot Sacramento Valley with determination, and it was superbly rewarding to arrive in fresh mountain air.

For three summers Aunt Alice and Mother took over their cous-ins Jack and Florence Walter's rambling estate called "Rampart," on the Truckee River. On the wooded grounds there were comfortably furnished tents for the boys or young houseguests, as well as the main, lodge-style house, where all of us sat down for meals together at the long refectory table that easily accommodated the crowd. That the long, rustic living room included a dining-room area was quite unusual for the time. There was a huge fireplace with hearth at the end of the room and a tremendous stuffed trout mounted on the wall, whose glassy eyes seemed to stare at me. Rampart was like a private resort, complete with playground, tennis court, and a big swimming hole down at the Truckee River. It was fun to float downstream and to climb over slippery rocks in order to cross over the river where it was shallow. I loved hiking along the river trail in the muffled hush of deep forest, and playing with my cousins every day—whisper-ing secrets and forming covert clubs. Once, in a secluded spot on the banks of the river, we wrote vows to one another in indelible ink. As part of our ritual we pricked our legs, creating a wound with the pen point. Then we became terrified that we might die of blood poisoning from the black ink mixed with the blood. We were greatly relieved to hear Mother's automobile rumbling across the wooden

Rampart bridge that served as an entrance to the estate. We rushed to confess our secret blood pact. Mother reassured us that we would not die, and gave us cotton soaked in alcohol with which to erase our indelible vows.

A retinue of servants accompanied us when we vacationed at Rampart, for it was a large enterprise. One summer when I was very young, I lived in mortal terror of the strict, militaristic Fräulein Annie, who tarnished what might otherwise have been happy memories. Fräulein Chassie, who had charge of my cousins, was far more permissive and fun loving. Part of our fun was the daily routine of rushing to meet the early-morning train. We would hear it whistling in the narrow gauge before it stopped at Rampart Station, where newspapers and mail were thrown off. Never will I forget the wrench of disappointment I experienced when Fräulein Annie would not allow me to meet the train with the other children because I could not fasten my high-button shoes in time to join the race to the train. I struggled in despair with those shoes and was never able to convey my feelings about Fräulein to Mother, who believed no ill of anyone. Every afternoon at three Aunt Alice and Mother ran down the road to the river, squealing with delight in their long black bathing suits, stockings, and tennis shoes. The grownups went swimming and fishing every day. Innumerable fishing rods, reels, baskets, bait, and waders were lined up on the porch, which we children were instructed never to touch. One night we had a moonlight picnic. Everyone was included, children and servants. A great bonfire was lit; we stood around it singing Gilbert and Sullivan songs and roasting marshmallows. The summer we spent at Rampart when I was nine years old, my nineteen-year-old brother, William, invited houseguests—two boys and three girls. I watched the girls enviously as they dressed for dinner. I can still see them tripping down the path wearing pale silk stockings that matched their dresses, rolled over elastic bands just above their knees. I thought this intriguingly daring. My cousins and I lurked behind screen doors peering at the six sophisticates unaware of our spying. It was a startling revelation to see my brother flirt. Once he played his portable Victrola and did a wild Charleston, kicking up his heels, with a petite partner, to the strains of "If You Like a Ukulele Lady." It seemed to me that my brother was another Fred Astaire.

There were summers at Tahoe Tavern when my parents permitted me to go without them as long as I was chaperoned by my aunt and uncle, and in the congenial company of my cousins. Aunt Alice was like a second mother to me, and I enjoyed sharing a room with Liz and Madeleine. Other members of the family trailed along, too. My aunt and uncle took over an entire wing of the old hotel for all of us. It took Aunt Alice a full day to get settled. On went her Hoover apron and, with the assistance of the chambermaid, Nellie, every drawer and closet was scrubbed with Fels-Naptha and papered before she would unpack her trunk. Soon her hotel room smelled as familiarly clean as her room at home. Every day she wrote to and received letters from my mother. Those were lovely Tahoe times: days of horseback-riding trips, icy dips in the lake, long walks along the lush lake trail, and movies and bowling in the casino at night.

One special summer when I was twelve years old, my uncle marshaled a group of a dozen of us to Alaska. Uncle Sam was a great leader, charting the trip, taking menu orders in the dining rooms, and attending to luggage. On that trip, he endeared himself to us so much that we nicknamed him "Dunkle," a combination of Dad and uncle. We sailed from Seattle on the *Dorothy Alexander,* and stopped at Vancouver and Victoria before taking the Inland Passage. I relished the idea that we were in a land of eternal sun and daylight. Perhaps we would never have to go to bed. The great icebergs floating close to the ship inspired my cousin Liz and me to secure a chunk as a souvenir. I was delegated to guard the piece of iceberg and kept our treasure in a water glass in my stateroom. Of course, it melted and one morning the chambermaid threw it out. Mother proved most inventive on this trip. Because we rebelled at eating a strong-tasting white root vegetable that looked like turnips, she concocted a convincing story about a newly discovered Alaskan vegetable called *rabis*. Beaming with enthusiasm, she assured us that Eskimos found *rabis* delicious and strengthening, a great guardian against the cold. For the remainder of the voyage we ate this dish with relish, fancying ourselves gourmet Eskimos preparing for the long snowbound winter. Back in San Francisco, the wonder vegetable became turnips again and far less palatable.

On the day we docked in Skagway, my cousin Billy and I "discovered gold." We went for a walk and came upon a gentleman who presented us with "nuggets" he claimed he had just mined. What excitement we experienced over our treasure! I kept my nugget for years after discovering we had been fooled, the subjects of a well-intentioned joke. In the town of White Horse, we were accosted by clouds of mosquitoes. The air was black with their density and resounded with buzzing as they circled around us. What intrigued me was how Mother and Aunt Alice lit cigarettes, believing the smoke would ward off the mosquitoes. Since neither of them smoked, it took ten minutes and much coughing before they achieved their objective. Holding the cigarette between thumb and second finger, they would take quick, anxious puffs, and then place the cigarette at arm's length, glaring at it with infinite distaste.

Believing it was time for their daughters to learn independence, the sisters shipped us off to a camp on Catalina Island for the remainder of the summer. Never before had I been away from home so long. I had never untangled my own long curls, I had never done my own laundry, and I had never kept myself or my clothes clean and in order. I loathed camp; I was homesick. I missed my mother's warmth, attention, and affection; her goodnight kiss. I missed the fun of being with her and my aunt, and I rebelled at the regimentation. I couldn't summon up the courage to dive into the ocean, so I was classified as a "minnow" instead of a "shark," and my activities were limited accordingly. For the entire session I never succeeded in being anything but a "minnow," whereas Liz and my sister achieved "shark" status. The happy day Mother and Aunt Alice came to take us home they listened tolerantly to my sad, shameful tale. I never went to camp again. Those few torturous weeks accomplished one thing: Mother finally allowed me to bob my hair so I could take care of it myself. I felt grown up and fashionable without my mass of baby curls.

Florine and Alice took trips to celebrate occasions, reasoning that if they were not in San Francisco no one could embarrass them with gifts or congratulations. On Mother and Father's silver anniversary, they took their children, Aunt Alice, Uncle Sam, and their entire brood to the luxurious Biltmore Hotel in Santa Barbara for the weekend. Mother sent out her original, leftover wedding invitations, merely altering the date and location. The evening of the anniversary, Mother surprised everyone by appearing in her wedding dress. It was so beautiful and romantic that although I was not able to do anything as lavish as to take an entourage to the Biltmore on my own twenty-fifth anniversary, I wore my bridal gown, just as Mother had done years before.

Once, to observe a birthday, Mother and Aunt Alice went to Las Vegas. They had never been to this reputedly wicked city of neon lights, gambling houses, and perpetual entertainment, and they wanted to go to the most exciting, risqué show they could find. True to form, they managed to secure seats next to the stage; they did not want to miss an undulation, an embrace, a trick, a high kick, or a naughty word. There they sat, with their eyes glued and their ears cocked. Mother put her purse down on a ledge so as not to be encumbered. There was a change of scenery, and quite suddenly the ledge vanished down into the bowels of the theater with the purse still on it. The theater was so constructed that the stage sank into a pit as another set rose. "Oh, my goodness!" Mother shrilled. "Where is my bag going?" Mother and her purse were the sensation of the show as the two sisters dissolved into conniptions such as Las Vegas had never witnessed before. Bent over with laughter, tears streaming down their faces, they stole the show.

Mother was more gregarious and less critical than Aunt Alice, who sometimes despaired at her sister's indiscriminate, all-embracing affection for everyone. Mother was quite shy with anyone she knew, but rather forward with strangers. She generally asked them questions, probing into their lives, and wondering aloud as to their love life. She managed to collect all sorts of people around her, both famous and infamous.

In 1952 San Francisco's Mayor Robinson organized a party to fly to Queen Elizabeth's coronation. Mother, who had been recently widowed and relatively homebound in preceding years, decided to go. She had neither traveled alone nor flown before. Seated next to her on a plane bound for London was a familiar-looking young man who appeared to be uncomfortable. Mother turned to him solicitously, proffering her silver pillbox. "Young man, have a Dramamine." She watched over him for the duration of the flight. The young man was the well-known Bay Area columnist Herb Caen. Despite the disparity in their ages, Mother and Herb struck up a fast friendship. After that trip, Caen occasionally appeared at Mother's Sunday-night dinners.

In 1959 my ten-year-old son John and I went to Europe with Mother. She enjoyed sitting in hotel lobbies where she could observe and sometimes chat with strangers. One afternoon in the lobby of the Hotel de la Paix in Geneva, John spotted his grandmother listening avidly to a suave gentleman who appeared to be propounding his innermost thoughts to her. As John approached, he heard the man extol life in Russia. Russia was the future, America was the past. Russia would triumph, America would flounder in capitalism. John was puzzled to see Mother nod her head in approval, agreeing, applauding, and interjecting remarks such as, "Isn't that marvelous? I never knew that...very interesting!" When the man took his most gracious leave, John asked his grandmother why she had listened so pleasantly to a Communist. "No, John, that's impossible," Mother insisted. "That man was much too nice. He couldn't possibly be a Communist."

Mother was then almost eighty years old, and a great sport on this European jaunt. She was eager to explore, to meet and chat with every sort of person, and like a magnet people gathered around her. One evening at a *hôtel dansant,* a courtly gentleman asked her to dance. "Oh, my dearie me, not I," she exclaimed. "You should dance with a young girl, like my daughter." I was forty-five years old at the time, but I was still a young girl in my mother's eyes. We spent a few days in Montana, high up in the Swiss Alps. Here at an ancient, old-fashioned resort, Mother, who was accustomed to every luxury and convenience, accepted a room without a bath. There was little for Mother to do in Montana, where you either hiked along steep, scenic trails or went horseback riding, so she challenged John to a game of ping-pong. These many years later, John has not recovered from his amazement: Mother beat him! We sailed home on the French liner *Le Flandre.* Mother was the belle of the ship and indulged herself in "people watching."

Coming or going, the sisters usually packed gifts for those at the other end. For many years, Aunt Alice's children Liz and Jim lived in Beverly Hills—which Aunt Alice seemed to think was a backwater. An ever-devoted mother, she visited them frequently, her arms laden with shrimp from San Francisco Bay, home-baked chocolate cake, loaves of sourdough bread, dozens of eggs, flowers from Atherton, and several pounds of seasonal vegetables. Once she traveled to Beverly Hills with her arms full of giant asparagus and other gastronomical gifts.

One day Mother suggested, "Allie, dear, let's go to Hong Kong to shop instead of Magnin's." So, in 1960, when Mother and Aunt Alice were both widows in their eighties, they jaunted off to the Orient with Connie and Woody Ong. The Ongs were conducting a tour through Japan, Hong Kong, Thailand, and Singapore. Prior to the trip, the Ongs had not been acquainted with the two elderly sisters, and were somewhat amazed that they chose to embark on such an energetic voyage. Connie was puzzled when the sisters stipulated that at all times, and in every place, each wished a single room with bath. She was under the logical impression that elderly sisters would prefer the security of being together in one room for the sake of economy and mutual companionship. Aunt Alice explained to Connie, "You see, dearie, every evening between five and six, I bathe. I must have my tub and that hour all to myself." This was Connie's first insight into the personalities she grew to know so well. Wherever she was in the world, Aunt Alice's bath was a firm, inflexible ritual. Mother was not quite so rigid as her sister; however, she too preferred privacy. In addition, she felt that Alice's preferences were quite perfect and something to emulate. Later, when Connie saw how the sisters lived in their own houses on Franklin Street, she could better understand their request for separate rooms. It must have been a strenuous journey for such elderly ladies, but the Ongs reported that they were the heart and soul of the journey and never, even on the hottest, most humid, tiring day was there ever a word of complaint from her two octogenarian travelers.

In the Orient, Mother and Aunt Alice had a fine opportunity to indulge their shopping mania. They pursued this pastime so ardently that in Hong Kong Mother ran out of money. She did not confide her situation to the Ongs, but frantically cabled her son Edward to mail the necessary funds. He did so immediately via American Express. The Ongs had set aside a day for the group to be at leisure. On the designated day, the Ongs ferried from the exclusive area of the Peninsula Hotel, where everyone was lodged, to the crowded, steaming business section. On the thronging streets in front of an imposing bank, the Ongs spotted Mother and Aunt Alice. The scene was startling. Behind the sisters stood a pair of turbaned Sikh guards holding rifles to their backs. Mother had an American Express cable grasped in her hand. She was waving it, pleading, trying to communicate, adamantly and indignantly demanding her money. The guards couldn't comprehend her English jabber. They had caught two criminal robbers and were about to arrest them. The Ongs came to the defense of the hapless sisters. Connie explained in Chinese that the two elderly American ladies were honorable and innocent members of a tour. Mother and Aunt Alice were freed from the rifle-thrust and Mother secured her money. Of course, the sisters happily scurried away to resume shopping. Aunt Alice and Mother returned home laden with silk coats and dresses, embroidered blouses and kimonos, colorful fans and party dresses, strings of Japanese cultured pearls, Sony radios, and innumerable oriental trinkets and souvenirs. A special taxi had to be engaged at San Francisco Airport to transport the load of paper butterflies Aunt Alice had purchased. Following this trip, the Ongs and their four small children were virtually adopted family. Ever afterwards they called the sisters Aunt Florine and Aunt Alice. From time to time they came to Sunday dinner or to a lunch and swim in the country, and on a Christmas Eve they were the only guests present who were not truly related. The sisters had six new names on their Christmas lists and in their birthday books.

Top left: Summertime in Atherton, about 1917. White linen dresses and fresh country air on the Peninsula. Left to right: Bertha Haas, Elizabeth Lilienthal, Rosalie Greenebaum (Bertha's mother), Frances Bransten, Florine Haas Bransten, Alice Haas Lilienthal, and Alice Bransten. **Middle left:** Tahoe Tavern, July 1930. **Bottom left:** Mule train, Lake Tahoe, early twentieth century. **Top right:** Florine on an amusement-park ride with her mother, Bertha Haas, circa 1905. **Middle right:** Billy Haas (brother of Madeleine Haas) with a big trout catch at "Rampart" on Truckee River, 1920s. **Bottom right:** Frances Lilienthal at Lake Tahoe, circa 1930.

Top left: "Allie, dear, let's go to Hong Kong instead of Magnin's." Alice and Florine and friend on a tour of the Orient in 1960. **Bottom left:** Alice (center) and Samuel with an unidentified woman on an ocean liner, 1920s. **Top right:** On their silver wedding anniversary in 1928, Edward and Florine hosted the entire family at the Biltmore Hotel in Santa Barbara for the weekend. Florine sent out her original, leftover wedding invitations, merely altering the date and location. **Middle right:** Alice Haas Lilienthal and Samuel Lilienthal (right) with son Ernest in upstairs front sitting room at 2007 Franklin Street, 1950s. **Bottom right:** Alice and Florine, seated foreground, celebrate Alice's seventy-fifth birthday with family in Las Vegas, 1960.

THE SISTERS IN WORLD WAR II

In their own inimitable way, the sisters fought World War II with heart and conscience. Although no longer young, they spent long hours rolling bandages at the Red Cross and serving coffee and dough-nuts to returning troops. Any lonely enlisted man was immediately invited to a home-cooked dinner. Soon assorted soldiers and sailors appeared at holiday dinners and were fussed, worried, and clucked over. The sisters stormed the portals of the blood bank, but as they were overage and underweight, they were continually rejected. They took up knitting socks and sweaters for "the boys" and spent many an evening muttering over dropped stitches and exchanging their work to assist one another in picking them up again. My husband, brother, and cousin were in the service. The sisters wrote daily letters to their sons; in their illegible penmanship, they covered the margins of Vic-tory letters and scribbled around the corners. I doubt that any censor ever succeeded in deciphering those hieroglyphics. They sent care packages to my husband, who was either on an undesignated Pacific atoll or on a ship in mid-Pacific, or to my cousin who was stationed in Florida. My brother Edward was an officer serving at Pearl Harbor.

For his birthday, Mother packed up a mammoth chocolate cake and shipped it off to Roger Cooper, a sailor friend stationed in the barracks at Pearl Harbor. She asked the seaman to please deliver the cake to my brother, a lieutenant, and surprise him by celebrating the day with him. Roger was obliged to hike up to officers' quarters carrying the box of squashed cake, complete with candles. Mother's loving determination surmounted even the U.S. wartime navy.

I, too, was the recipient of gifts during the war. The sisters preserved barrels of eggs in what seemed to me a nauseating pickling fluid. They gave me a barrel, presumably to bake with. But as I never baked, I stored the barrel away in the basement and threw it out at the end of the war. I was presented with a huge and weighty firebomb extinguisher which I could never fasten to any of the plaster walls in my apartment. This I stuffed away in a closet for the duration. I received huge bolts of black sateen with which I was to whip up the required blackout curtains. The material was elegant, but I was not handy with measurements, needles, and thread. I substituted dark, old army blankets, and kept the sateen for future Halloween drapery, but I cannot recall if I accomplished that either. In any case, my mother and aunt hovered over me solicitously during my husband's absence. Had I permitted it, they would have given me half of their ration stamps. When V-J day finally came, the whole world was elated and thankful for the promise of peace, but awed by the horror and potential of the atomic bomb. Shopping was still uppermost in Aunt Alice's mind. My husband, Hans, would be coming home after four long years of dreadful Pacific warfare, frontline invasions, kamikaze attacks, bouts with dengue fever, and life and death on isolated atolls. Aunt Alice was overjoyed for me and telephoned her delight. "Dearie," she suggested, "why not ask your Hans to get permission to come home via China? They have the most unusual gold bracelets there. I'd like some for all the girls in the family. And in Hong Kong

he can buy English cashmeres. I'll just make a list of sizes and preferred colors. Liz looks lovely in green, that's size twelve....Madeleine
in blue, size ten...." I had to interrupt and explain that my husband
was no place near China or Hong Kong; he would be shipped home
with his field hospital and there would be no shops en route. The
sisters accepted this explanation and began making jubilant plans for
his homecoming.

As Aunt Alice and Mother were born romantics, they never
wanted to miss witnessing a love scene, a reunion, or an embrace.
As the time grew closer for Hans's return, Mother telephoned me to
inquire if I knew where she and Aunt Alice could purchase chicken
wire. Accustomed as I was to their eccentric shopping pursuits, this
request completely baffled me. "You see, darling, Aunt Alice and I
plan to erect bushes in your apartment. We want to put up chicken
wire. We'll hang bundles of green branches through the wire, and
then we'll hide behind the bushes so we can see how your Hans
greets his children when he comes in the front door." I could not
refuse this plea that came from their hearts. That evening I was to call
for my husband at Fort Bragg. My mother and Aunt Alice insisted
that I be chauffeured, because I might be too excited to drive safely
and so that I would have time for a relaxed, private reunion. Hans
and I arrived home. Of course, I knew where Alice and Mother were
concealed. Hans was too immersed in the emotion of the moment to
notice how unusual it was to have trees both growing and swaying in
our apartment, or to hear the children giggling self-consciously and
the suppressed "shhh" sound in the air. He did not seem too amazed
when the ladies emerged from behind their bushes, completely gratified by their stunt, exploding in laughter and tears. After years in the
family, he, too, was aware of the endearing idiosyncrasies of Mother
and Aunt Alice.

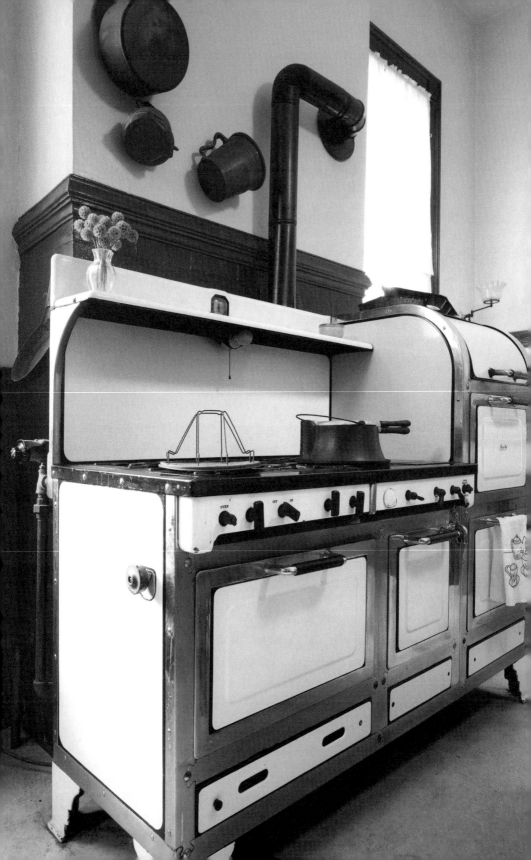

ALL IN AN AVERAGE DAY: THE SIXTIES

◇◇

The pattern and tempo of Aunt Alice's and Mother's life altered very little with the passage of time. In the 1960s, the sisters lived and thought in much the same manner as they had in the 1920s. As elderly ladies with all their children gone from home, they remained amid their many empty rooms, each in her own Franklin Street house, attended by a variety of servants whom they never ceased to worry about and cater to. They continued to have Sunday and holiday dinners, to walk downtown on shopping expeditions, to telephone and visit back and forth, to shop for gifts galore, and to run all manner of errands. They clung to their ideas and ideals, and expressed these in their same particular phraseology. On their walks they would bow to those with whom they had merely a nodding acquaintance. Mother still said, when aggravated, "I could just jump out of my skin," but nevertheless she remained intact. She continued to mutter such shockers as "Oh, ding it all!" or "Oh, shoot!" The sisters also persisted in taking home attractive articles they spotted in a store "on approval." "Young lady," they would address the worried saleswoman, whether she was young or old, "don't you know, things look entirely different when you have them at home than they do on display?" Although now Mother had need of a chauffeur, there were days when the sisters ventured out alone, and the report was, "Aunt Alice took the wheel." The enthusiastic cry to describe their outing might be, "Such a good time, it was quite beyond measure!" If it were a hot day, Mother would fan herself vigorously, declaring, "It's a hitzer-vitzer," which seemed to be a language all her own. Her grandchildren have inherited this "Mother-invented" phrase, their inflection an exact echo. Again, Mother might well intone, "It's as hot as all get-out!"

Although the sisters' lives, activities, conversations, and values remained intact for half a century, there were a few minor adjustments, such as an occasional meat purchase at "that really lovely Grant Market on Market Street," as a change from ordering from Joe Hermann, or going to a beauty parlor in place of having Miss Harder and Annie Quinn come to the house to have their hair washed and nails done. Most things, however, remained unchanged. Time dimmed their eyes and ears, to a degree. They now needed eyeglasses to read or do handiwork, and they began to accuse people of mumbling, "not speaking clearly," or "not enunciating properly." When they finally yielded to hearing aids, they rarely used them; they thought them unnecessary, "if people would just talk up."

On a certain day, Mother complained to Aunt Alice that she must have her eyes reexamined, and her glasses altered. The lenses seemed all wrong. Aunt Alice remarked on an amazing coincidence. She had the same complaint. Together they marched down to their oculist in the Fitzhugh Building on Union Square. Dr. Hosford got out his charts, peered into Mother's eyes, and looked carefully at her eyeglasses. He then asked to see Aunt Alice's glasses. He cleared his throat with some embarrassment. "My dear Mrs. Bransten, if you would wear your own eyeglasses instead of your sister's, I believe the situation would correct itself." As may be surmised, the sisters dissolved into fits of laughter. They frequently took one another's eye-glasses by error; it came to a point where they scarcely trusted each other and were constantly accusing the other one of just that. One could count on Mother mislaying her glasses almost daily. She would say, "I've lost my glasses again. I'll bet Aunt Alice took them as usual. Please dial her and ask." Aunt Alice would be indignant, as though this were something unheard of. We finally gave Mother a ribboned necklace on which to attach her glasses, but this didn't help, nor did several pairs of extra glasses. She managed to misplace them all simultaneously.

When I. Magnin's enlarged and moved from its cozy old Grant Avenue premises to Geary Street, I went to the opening with Mother and Aunt Alice. They were in awe of the gilded marble restroom, the crystal fixtures sparkling from ceilings, and the expansive ele-gance of thick wall-to-wall carpeting, but they lamented the loss of the smaller, more informal quarters where they knew every inch and every employee. One day the sisters decided to explore the Ranleigh and the Marima departments to see the merchandise of these less-costly floors. In the Marima, they spotted a five-dollar knit stocking hat and lunged at it in excitement. It seemed just the same shade as an expensive dress Aunt Alice had purchased on the exclusive second floor. They grabbed the hat to take it into better light, and on further thought, they decided to go directly to the second floor with it and compare it to the dress. Tugging it back and forth between them, enthusiastically engrossed in animated conversation as to its color and merits, they walked to the elevator. A harried salesgirl spotted them removing the merchandise. Vivian Seeay, a close friend of mine, was then assistant to the merchandise manager. Fortunately Vivian happened to be in the Marima at that very moment. The alarmed salesgirl rushed up to Vivian. "Mrs. Seeay, those old ladies just stole a hat. I don't know what to do. See, they're leaving with it, over there by the elevator. Hadn't you best speak to them, or call the house detective?" Vivian recognized my mother and Aunt Alice. "Dear girl," she consoled, "those two ladies aren't thieves. They are perhaps a bit eccentric, but utterly charming, and completely harmless. They could buy any hat in Magnin's they wanted." Vivian hurried over to greet the sisters, and patiently to discuss the color of the hat with them in minute detail. Once again, in San Francisco as in Hong Kong, Mother and Aunt Alice were rescued from being apprehended.

Mother and Aunt Alice wished to keep abreast of the times, and together they attended civic events and world-affairs lectures. Usually they contrived to be seated in the very first row because they noted that speakers did not "speak up" as they had in former years. One evening in the Veterans Auditorium where a world-renowned lecturer was to speak, the podium was centered so that the audience could gather around the speaker as advantageously as possible. Of course the sisters politely but determinedly shoved their way into seats next to the lectern. In the middle of the engrossing talk, Mother stood up, took the pitcher from the conveniently placed lectern, poured herself a glass of water, drank eagerly, and sat down again, gratified. I was not present, but a friend, Richard Sloss, witnessed Mother's performance. At first he was too stupefied to note the speaker's reaction or whether there was a stunned pause, but when he recognized my mother, he was not surprised by her consistently natural behavior. "Why," she might ask, "would there be water if it wasn't to drink?" Through the years, Richard never tired of telling this tale of Mother's astonishing aplomb, but he'd add, "She thanked the speaker most audibly and graciously." Mother was always puzzled as to why this story was amusing.

With the passing years, Mother and Aunt Alice paid calls on their grandchildren as well as their children. It was a delight to see them

come, a disappointment to see them go. It was not unusual for Mother to walk into my house, announcing that it was time for her to leave. She perched on the edge of a chair, wailing, "I'm so faint, I'm starving. Please give me a dry piece of bread. No, nothing on it; no, no butter, just a crust!" She devoured the bread as she stood, ready to leave. Breathing a sigh of satisfaction, she would say, "Absolutely delicious! Lucky I stopped by. I was so ravenous, and that's just what I wanted!"

Mother and Aunt Alice ate heartily, and never left a scrap on a plate; they raved about something as simple as mashed potatoes with the appreciation due a gourmet dish. Once, for their lunch, I scrambled some eggs. They were absolutely rhapsodic about my culinary abilities. "How do you know how to scramble eggs so beautifully?" they asked, lost in admiration. They were equally impressed by the accompanying rye toast that I was able to make pop up from the automatic toaster. There was no ordinary thing that any of their children did that was not completely marvelous. Once, as Mother watched her daughter-in-law Sue straighten out her son's crib, she applauded her dexterity and talent. "How do you do it, Sue? That's just wonderful." Another day when Mother was paying a call, one of her grandchildren, aged fourteen, emerged from a bath. Mother, impressed and enraptured, exclaimed, "Do you mean to tell me that you are able to take a bath all by yourself?" One evening the sisters dined at my house; as usual, they raved about everything I served. When I brought out the *pièce de résistance,* Aunt Alice asked, "Where did you get this lemon pie?" as she ate it with apparent relish. "Blum's," I replied. "No wonder," she stated disapprovingly. "That's why it tastes so artificially sweetened and rubbery. Home-baked pies are so much better. Don't you agree?" Homemade was always considered superior! A visit to the children's supper hour occasioned Mother to remark in surprise, "I didn't know that milk came in boxes!" Later, when my child asked, "Hasn't Grandma ever seen milk in a carton?" I explained that on Franklin Street milk had never been placed on the table in its container.

Improbable as it may sound, Mother had the following conversation with one of her nieces. "You know, dearie, I heard you being conceived!" My flabbergasted cousin asked, "What do you mean, Aunt Florine?" "Well," Mother explained, "some years back Ed and I went on a weekend trip with your parents. We had adjacent rooms. In the middle of the night I heard their bed squeaking and nine months later you were born. So you see, I heard your conception. Isn't that lovely?"

Top left: Florine and Alice at 2007 Franklin Street, Christmas 1968. **Top right**: Alice greets family connection Cindy Matzger on Christmas at 2007 Franklin Street, 1971. **Bottom**: Alice and Florine at Atherton, 1960s.

Top left: Alice at Atherton, 1950s. Top right: The two sisters captured by a street photographer shopping in downtown San Francisco. Bottom: Alice and Florine in Japan, 1960, giggling as usual.

THE CYCLE OF TIME

There are repetitive echoes in the cycle of time that create a feeling of continuation. Memory rekindles the spark of a vibrant personality who died years ago; one seems to hear that voice, see a characteristic movement, sense a vital presence. Memory links generation to generation in such a way as to perpetuate life and immortality. My grandmother's Franklin Street house symbolized to me an integral part of her personality. Just so do my children recall their grandmother's house; they experience it as a vital essence imbued with her identity. They, too, in their memories, hear sounds that have never stilled, smell aromas that were never stifled, see settings never eclipsed, and touch certain things, the feel of which time never numbed.

Tangible objects and special toys illuminate my recollection of happy hours absorbed in play at 2007 Franklin Street. On the second floor in the back hall was an organ, currently residing in the front hall. Pulling out all the stops, pressing down full force on the pedals, and pounding mercilessly on the keys, I pretended to be a great musician, as sounds bellowed and swelled with harsh dissonance. In the dining room, on a side table, stood a shining samovar. I liked fiddling with its faucet, turning it round and round. I enjoyed looking at the sparkling wine glasses and luminous chinaware enclosed within glass cabinets. Grandma's huge marble bathroom fascinated me. Here stood a small, low tub and I wondered who could squeeze into such an awkwardly shaped basin. What was its purpose when there was a fine, large bathtub adjacent, standing high on metallic legs? I was brusquely told that the little tub was a "foot bath." It was many years before I discovered that the "foot bath," to my Victorian elders, was an unmentionable bidet. In the attic was a standard-gauge Lionel electric train that ran in an enormous layout along intricate tracks, through tunnels, up hills, and around curves, making a breathtaking loop-the-loop. The train belonged to my cousin Billy Haas. It was exciting to watch Billy and his friends play with it. The boys raced the train so that it veered off the tracks. One of their games was to see how far the cars could fly into the room; another was to reverse switches so that there would be a great collision. In the nursery there was a dollhouse inhabited by miniature Victorian people. There was the mother with her pompadour; the father with his Van Dyke, swallowtail coat, and dove-gray vest; a girl with curls and starched petticoated dress, and a boy with knickers, jacket, and bow tie. There was a black-uniformed maid in white cap and apron, a rotund, jolly-looking cook holding a mixing spoon, a white-waisted, black-skirted nursemaid, a tiny kitten, and a leashed puppy. Each room was furnished in minute detail—from paintings on the walls to a sideboard with a nosegay of flowers and candlesticks gracing it; the table was set with Lilliputian china and silver. The bathroom was well equipped and remarkably detailed, so much so that a long gold chain hung from the toilet. The cook looked ready to light the black iron stove, the father seemed ready to sharpen his razor and shave from a tiny enamel basin, the kitten to meow, the puppy to bark, the maid to dust, the mother to read to the children—having tossed her microscopic needlepoint aside on a chair—while the nursemaid reached to empty the chamber pot. Cousin Liz was the lucky owner and custodian of this heirloom dollhouse. She treasured it, and although I was permitted to gaze at it for rhapsodic minutes, I was not allowed to touch anything. I looked at it with my hands behind my back as Liz touched a switch illuminating all the rooms in the dollhouse; the ornate crystal chandelier suspended from the ceiling in the parlor twinkled magically.

Memories of my grandmother's Victorian home are tied together in a fairy-tale binding. How well I recall afternoon visits when I felt like a veritable princess. Walking along Franklin Street as I approached the house, I gazed up in awe of the turrets, gables, and pointed tower. As I entered through the lace-curtained front door, I alternately sank into thick rugs or clicked across shining hardwood floors. Old paintings in ornate gilt frames fascinated me, as did the gleaming copper and brass ornaments. Once up the stairway and past the newel post into Grandmother's talcum-scented sanctuary, I bestowed a dutiful peck on her withered, sweet-smelling cheek, anxious to hurry to my favorite haunt, the attic, which was neatly stacked with ancient trunks. I was permitted to rifle through the top trunk where Grandmother had carefully stored her old gowns, silks, and satins adorned with laces and ruffles. The only difficulty I had was with the many hooks, eyes, and buttons. I happily wrestled into a gown, placed an old plumed hat onto my bobbed hair, and rummaged until I found a tattered beaded bag or fan. I made my way to the one window in the attic tower where I posed for a few minutes and gazed down on Franklin Street, looking for the prince who should be approaching on a white stallion. After enacting that scenario, I carefully descended to my grandmother's chamber, where she waited to applaud my costume. We shared a ceremonious tea as I fanned myself extravagantly, extended my pinkie finger from the cup's handle, and rolled my eyes in the manner of a proper princess. We chatted about the ball I was to attend with a prince that evening, and about the many princes who would come to woo me. At last, filled with romantic visions and delicious cookies, I bade my grandmother adieu, tripped from her room, and went to the attic to disrobe, and divest myself of an afternoon dream with my wonderful ally. "Bye, Grandma," I called as I loped down the stairs in my Oxfords. Rushing down Franklin Street, I was once again an eleven-year-old in the reality of 1925.

Fortunately for me and everyone else, Grandmother's house lived on after she died, graced and blessed by the exceptional personalities of Aunt Alice, Uncle Sam, and their children. Life resumed. The grandfather clock toned away the hours, the brasses gleamed, flowers crowded vases, delicious aromas continued to waft from the kitchen, and familiar voices caressed the walls. My daughter, Susan, enjoyed precious visits with her grandmother Florine just as I had had with mine. During the 1940s, Hans and I lived in an apartment on the corner of Jackson and Franklin Streets. I watched six-year-old Susan from the window as she made her way down Franklin Street with an overnight bag clutched in her hand, dutifully looking both ways at intersections, bound for an overnight trip to her grandmother's house. These excursions continued until Susan was in her teens and went away to college. Her memories are permeated with love. Mother initiated Susan into the feminine arts of needlepoint and knitting and gave her her first piano lessons. On one unforgettable occasion, my mother took Susan to the main branch of the Wells Fargo Bank. There, amid iron vaults, marble floors, uniformed security guards, and the cold formality of an institution, little Susan was led by her determined grandmother. The manager appeared and inquired solicitously if he could be of help. Mother took out her bank statement to say, "Look at this, dearie. You are a smart young man. You add this up yourself. You will find this statement is incorrect. I'm afraid your nice bank is five cents off." Surprisingly enough, Mother was right!

Susan's memories of overnight visits at Franklin Street are crowded with tactile images. She treasured her tête-à-têtes with her grandmother right before bedtime, when my mother appeared in her pink corduroy bathrobe, her hair neatly braided. Susan loved the soft feel and sweet scent of her grandmother's robe, and asked me to shop for a duplicate so she could look and smell just like her grandmother. Exploring Mother's bedroom, Susan lived through sensory adventures similar to mine as a child. She examined many objects on the great mahogany bureau: the pincushion stabbed full of ornate hatpins, some of which shone with jewels; the tiny silver box with etched figures in which Mother kept her stamps; the embossed silver nail buffer with matching buttonhook, the perfume bottle, the ornamental hand mirror and clothes brush. Mother kept a large glass-and-silver box stuffed with fragrant rose leaves and a small one filled with tongue-biting mints called *Carmeliten Pfeffermintz*. These tiny mints, imported from Germany, were a longtime favorite of the sisters. Whenever Mother and Alice went to the theater, the mints were placed in silver pillboxes, brought along, and offered to me during the performance. Scattered in nooks were the sachets that had been a summer project. Mother and Aunt Alice had picked bushels of fragrant lavender when they were in Atherton. Working at a table on the terrace, they filled silk bags with the fragrant buds, sewing them and tying them together with ribbons. Mother's lingerie—the chemises and stiffly laced corsets in the second drawer of the bureau—gave out the spicy aroma of lavender. Of course, the corsets were of interest to a child because they evoked the past in a very real way. Mother took her corsets of circa 1900 to Frieda Morrill, a specialty shop on Polk Street, and had them duplicated as exactly as possible. She would have "no truck" with modern girdles.

My son John has warm memories of his grandmother that rival Susan's. Sometimes Mother invited John and his cousin Peter to dinner. On one such evening Mother concluded dinner with, "I'll call the chauffeur to take you boys to the movies. Here is ten dollars." The amount far exceeded admission to the movies. John gulped, "Grandma, we don't need that much money." "Oh, yes, I want you to go to Blum's afterwards and have a *nice* ice cream soda." John shrank in embarrassment and wondered what James, the chauffeur, would do while they were at a movie, and wondered how he and Peter could spend the remainder of that vast sum on ice cream. Unable to combat my mother's enthusiastic persistence, the boys were driven away rolling in new wealth and feeling like embarrassed millionaire potentates.

There are many times when I sense a perpetuation of the personalities and spirit of Mother and Aunt Alice. Their conviviality and delight in celebration have infected all with whom they had contact. Tomorrow is the Fourth of July. I, now a member of the older generation, am invited to Atherton with my children and grandchildren. The sisters will not be there in their white straw hats and summer voiles, giggling and knitting by the pool, but I know we will speak of them. We always do. I know I will sense the rich inheritance, that imperishable warmth, hospitality, and spirit of festivity, which Aunt Alice left indelibly on her niece, the present hostess, my cousin Madeleine. It is not only at special events that I hear and feel echoes in time. The sisters endowed their children and grandchildren with something of mood, interaction, value, speech, and inflection. Tomorrow, my cousin Madeleine will apologize over a superb meal, stating, "It isn't quite as good as it should be." She will watch over every guest's comfort. The dining area will be decorated patriotically, and Beau, the small bichon frise, will sport red, white, and blue ribbons on his head. Liz will be there, crinkling her eyes with laughter in the same merry manner of Aunt Alice's. Madeleine, Liz, and I will sit by the pool, chatting and watching the younger ones in the water. We will feel that we look and sound like Aunt Alice and Mother in years past. As her guests depart, Madeleine will present each of us with a dozen fresh eggs and a box brimming with summer fruits. Her understated, generous gesture will be strikingly reminiscent of Aunt Alice's.

In these many ways, the past is perpetuated. The spirit of the sisters will never die. Today, Franklin Street and Atherton reverberate with echoes of the past. I look back with love to that "once upon a time," to the adventures and misadventures of the sisters: their giggles, scolds, endearing eccentricities, their unique relationship. I look back with happy nostalgia to family gatherings, dinners, parties; above all, the whole gamut of lives so abounding in warmth, generosity, and verve. Mother and Aunt Alice have left an indelible imprint on the cycle of time.

Top left: Frances Rothmann and children, Billy and Susan, 1940s. **Middle left:** Frances Rothmann, early 1940s. **Bottom left:** Frances and son John Rothmann, 1949. **Top right:** Florine with daughter Frances and grandchildren Susan and Billy, 1940s. **Bottom right:** Four generations, left to right: Arianne and Susan (Rothmann) Abrami, Frances (Bransten) Rothmann, and Florine (Haas) Bransten, 1960.

Top left: "In the attic was a standard-gauge Lionel electric train that ran in an enormous layout along intricate tracks, through tunnels, up hills, and around curves, making a breathtaking loop-the-loop." It belonged to Billy Haas, and was set up by the chauffeur, Morton Vrang. **Middle left:** Travel trunks in the attic, 1972. **Bottom left:** The dining room at 2007 Franklin Street, 1972, the year the house was transferred to San Francisco Heritage. **Top right:** Golden-oak sideboard and built-in cabinetry in the dining room at 2007 Franklin Street, 1972. **Bottom right:** Upstairs master bathroom at 2007 Franklin Street, 1972 (probably updated in 1898).

EPILOGUE

Mother and Aunt Alice lived in a tranquil, protected segment of time. They grew up in an isolated chapter of history: between the mid-nineteenth century, when Jews who sought freedom from persecution and the right to further their fortunes emigrated from Germany to America, and the mid-twentieth century, when the Holocaust raged through Europe. The sisters never knew the rigors of immigration, never felt the flames of extermination, and were never lashed by hate, vituperation, or intolerance.

In 1862, their father, William Haas, then a young boy, uprooted himself from his home in Reckendorf, Bavaria, and came to America with his brother Abraham. The boys were welcomed by Kalman and Charles, two cousins who had preceded them. Migration was a result of the conditions that followed the fateful revolutions of 1848 and had profound repercussions in Germany. My grandmother, Bertha Greenebaum Haas, was born and raised in San Francisco. My great-grandparents, Rosalia Cauffman Greenebaum and Hermann Greenebaum, both came to America as children. Aunt Alice's and Mother's ties were thoroughly American. They grew up in a culturally integrated world; their parents and grandparents assimilated the customs and rituals of Christian Americans. There was no discernable anti-Jewish prejudice during the early years in San Francisco.

Pioneer Jews attained civic distinctions; they were welcomed and respected for their cultural, philanthropic, and civic contributions. They were accepting and accepted. Mother and Aunt Alice's innocence and naiveté reflected the sheltered world they grew up in—one of respected, wealthy, upper-class Jews. Grandfather Haas, a native German and a Jew with a long tradition of Jewish customs ingrained in him, became a leader of both the Jewish and Gentile communities, as did my paternal grandfather, Joseph Brandenstein, and my uncle Sam's father, Ernest Reuben Lilienthal.

They celebrated Christmas and Easter rather than Chanukah and Pesach/Passover because these were the holidays of the culture they lived in. They joined exclusive clubs and sent their children to select schools, which in later years exerted stricter ratios of race and religion. There was always a quota for Jews in certain special clubs and schools, but before World War I there was a minimum of anti-Semitism in San Francisco. A letter my uncle H. U. Brandenstein wrote to a nephew in 1929 states in part:

> The San Francisco Verein, later called the Argonaut (founded in 1864) was primarily a German club (founded in 1853), and very exclusive at that: exclusive on the proper lines, admitting only gentlemen and men of education. Later the Germans withdrew and it became a Jewish institution, changing its name to Argonaut.

Although the sisters grew up in San Francisco's Christian culture with its rituals, festivals, and social customs, they were proudly loyal to their Jewish origins. No longer the devout synagogue Jews of the old world, they became philanthropic organizational Jews of the new world. They supported and served in Jewish causes with devotion. Their actions did not preclude generosity to and interest in worthy Christian causes and charities. They gave to the United Crusade as well as to the Jewish Federation. Grandfather Haas opened his home to all his nephews who came from Germany, and Mother often related how there seldom was time when a German cousin was not boarding at 2007 Franklin Street or working at Haas Brothers Wholesale Grocery. Grandfather kept in constant touch with sisters and brothers who remained in Germany. Through the years he traveled on transatlantic steamers to visit them with his wife and children. Later, Grandfather Haas sent funds abroad so that those who wished could settle in the United States. He found suitable husbands and provided dowries for his sisters and half sisters.

Mother and Aunt Alice sent their children to Sunday religious school and had reserved seats at Temple Emanu-El. Although they did not attend services regularly and could not persuade their recalcitrant husbands to accompany them, they never missed High Holy Day services and they attended memorial services at designated times. The sisters knew little about Jewish rites. The menorahs, (traditional candelabras) adorning their Franklin Street houses were merely artifacts ornamenting their dining and living rooms. We might dine on gorgeously glazed hams, but Mother worried endlessly about our Catholic nurse's Lenten diet. These were not intentional or prejudicial defiances; they were merely a part of the world the sisters knew and lived in. Of course, they had heard about old Jewish traditions, but they were felt to be part of a different world, a world of old *tantes* living in backwards Bavarian villages. Mother spoke to me about one of these old aunts who refused to light her fire against the bitter cold because of the Sabbath. Her account sounded foreign and fascinating, as though she were speaking of unknown customs on a faraway planet.

As a child I never heard Aunt Alice or mother use words such as *yahrzeit, shiva, mikveh,* or *chuppah.* Although married by rabbis, their weddings and the weddings of their children took place in homes, gardens, and hotels—not in synagogues. When my first son, Billy, was born at Lenox Hill Hospital in New York and I was asked when the bris was to take place, I replied, "I just nursed him a half hour ago." I believed the nurse who made inquiry of me lisped and mispronounced *breast* as *bris;* it seemed to me that she was asking me when the baby was to be fed again.

Many of our dead were cremated. My father, however, was buried, not because of my mother's identification with Judaism but because of her feeling that cremation was too final and obliterating. On the first anniversary of Father's death, she instinctively took my small daughter Susan along to the cemetery, where she planted two small rosebushes at father's graveside: a gesture of love, not one prescribed by Jewish ritual.

Although all the boys in our family were circumcised, this was looked upon as medical procedure and was privately performed by a physician; it was not seen as religious ritual with accompanying festivities and celebration. I never heard of the word *circumcision* until I was grown. It was considered taboo by the Victorian sisters because it dealt with a personal, physical matter.

Grandfather Brandenstein was born in the village of Hume, near Cassel, Germany, in 1827. Grandmother and Grandfather Brandenstein joined Temple Emanu-El, but I do not believe they were strict ritualists, although they observed the fast on Yom Kippur. Grandmother was more religiously observant than Grandfather, but she catered to him, so that if he wanted to eat Westphalian ham, she found redemption by not watching him as he ate. Little Janet Jacobi, a granddaughter, once asked, "What is a Jew?" The answer came back, "Someone who tells the truth and believes in God." Grandfather Brandenstein, although not a traditionalist, was an involved Jew. He served on the directorate of the Pacific Hebrew Orphan Asylum and as president of the Mt. Zion Hospital Association. He was a San Francisco civic leader as well as a prominent Jewish leader. In 1876, he was the president of the German Benevolent Society. He not only selected the site of the German hospital, also known as Franklin Hospital (now a branch of California Pacific Medical Center) but also put up the funds for the purchase of the lands. He was a founder of the German "Altenheim," an elder-care facility, and served as its president for several terms. Grandfather Haas was a valued member of Congregation Emanu-El. Like Grandfather Brandenstein, he served as the president of Mt. Zion Hospital. He, too, undertook many civic and social responsibilities. He was a director of Wells Fargo Bank and a member of the San Francisco Chamber of Commerce. Over the years he held other positions of honor and responsibility in his adopted city. Mother and Aunt Alice were imbued with the principles of charity and love. Their elders provided a constant example of philanthropic Judaism and generosity towards all. Their husbands, my father and Uncle Sam, were also sympathetic and loyal to their friends and community. Both were active businessmen who ignored Jewish ritual, but nevertheless found time and heart to serve their coreligionists. Father was a member of the Federation of Jewish Charities and served as a director of Mt. Zion Hospital. He gave liberally to Jewish causes and was a source of affidavits for refugees fleeing religious persecution.

Father had indomitable feelings of loyalty. His allegiance and fidelity towards fellow Jews were stern, resolute, and ideologically active. In 1920, Henry Ford published a series of blatantly anti-Semitic articles in the *Dearborn Independent* entitled "The International Jew: The World's Foremost Problem." Father never forgave him. He boycotted Ford's automobiles for the rest of his life, and would not even glance at the lukewarm apology Ford wrote to the Jewish community in the late 1920s. On my eighteenth birthday, in 1932, my parents indulged me with a surprise gift: a cream-colored Chevrolet convertible, complete with rumble seat. The Chevrolet was almost a symbol of defiance. My contemporaries might get around in their flashy tin lizzies, but spotting a Ford on the street was a personal insult to Father. After World War I affluent Jews invested in fancy cars imported from Germany, but it infuriated Father. He despised the American hero Charles Lindbergh. After Lindbergh's America First rally in September 1941, Father never wished to hear his name mentioned. He never forgave Lindbergh's statement that the Jews, the British, and the Roosevelt administration were the cause of many American ills, and that the war was caused by the Jews. Father was unwavering in all his principles and ideas. He did not countenance divorce and lost respect for President Roosevelt solely because of the divorces among the Roosevelt children. Father was fiercely proud when a Jew attained distinction. His face shone and his shoulders straightened when he spoke of Justice Brandeis, a Jew appointed to the Supreme Court. He was very aware of the great and good deeds that Jews had performed. In ideological spheres, Father identified with his fellow Jews.

Uncle Sam supported and served several Jewish causes. He was a founder of the *Jewish Community Bulletin* and served as its treasurer. He served as president of the Federation, and was a treasurer of the Jewish Community Relations Council. Uncle Sam and Father left rich legacies and examples of right living both as Americans and as Jews.

My family moved in a close, limited circle. Cousins intermarried frequently because these young people mingled with and were introduced to family members. Uncle Sam and Aunt Alice were second cousins. Liz and Jim Gerstley are distant cousins. When I had a date with a boy, Father invariably tried to pinpoint him within this close circle. I recall cringing in embarrassment when Father whispered loudly in front of the boy, "What did you say his name is? Who are his parents? Where does he come from?" If he were the son of a known San Francisco Jew with a familiar name and standing in the community, Father would beam and nod, not due to any snobbery, but because the familiar was comfortable and safe. My parents seldom extended themselves socially beyond the particular circle of Jewish friends and relatives they had always known. When Liz and Jim were engaged, Uncle Sam gave a sigh of relief and remarked, "I'm glad I don't have to meet new family." This, of course, was half jest, but only half—for it was comforting that Jim's English family and Sam were both related and acquainted. My mother was indeed most open-hearted socially, but constant, actual social intercourse was limited and repetitive.

During the 1940s a rebirth of religion swept through America. Jews especially sought to recover their lost identities and flourish anew, for they had suffered through the Holocaust. Six million Jews had been exterminated in Hitler's gas chambers; among these six million were relatives. Aunt Alice and Uncle Sam were members of the American Council for Judaism; they were ardent anti-Zionists. I remember their motto: "We're Americans first: to be Jewish is our religion and has nothing to do with our nationality." Times and loyalties had radically changed by the time Uncle Sam died, in 1957. One day I ventured to ask Aunt Alice why she still belonged to the Council. Her answer is typical of the sisters: "Because Uncle Sam did." She listened with interested amazement to opposing arguments, because what her Sam did was always right. Mother and Aunt Alice nearly always felt, voted, and followed in the footsteps of their husbands. Mother rebelled only once in her life, when she voted for Woodrow Wilson, in 1916, because he promised peace. She could straddle an issue with irrational compromise, joining both the American Council for Judaism and Hadassah simultaneously. She found this logical and justifiable, although the two organizations are diametrically opposed in philosophy. She claimed they were both "right." In any case, she wished to spare feelings and keep peace in the family by championing both and agreeing with everybody.

Mother's and Aunt Alice's sons followed in the tradition of serving Jewish and civic causes. My brother William was president of the Federation of Jewish Charities while a very young man. Ernest Lilienthal is a past president of the Bureau of Jewish Education. He has been on the board of Homewood Terrace, the Jewish orphanage, as a director and as its president, as had been his father. He has been on the board of the Jewish Community Center and the Jewish Welfare Federation. He is a past president of the local chapter of the American Technion Society, a position my brother Edward has also held. Ernest is a vice-president of the San Francisco Board of Trade and chairman of the board of Haas Brothers. He has returned to the fold, to some degree, inasmuch as he is a devoted member of Temple Emanu-El; he kindles the Chanukah lights, and when his daughters were small he observed Jewish festivals.

In the late 1970s, the president of the American Technion Society was William Russell-Shapiro, Madeleine's son-in-law. He also served as a vice-president of the American Jewish Congress and is very involved in community affairs. He has followed Madeleine's outstanding participation in community life. Among Madeleine's numerous involvements has been her active participation on behalf of both the Hebrew University in Jerusalem and Brandeis University in Massachusetts. My brother Edward has served many Jewish organizations with dedication and devotion. He has been chairman of the Jewish Community Relations Council and of the local chapter of the American Jewish Committee; he has also been on the board of Mount Zion Hospital. Edward currently has the honor of being a commissioner for the San Francisco Public Library. Edward and Ernest have traveled extensively in Israel under various auspices. My brother William's wife, Sue, is on numerous Jewish boards: that of the American Jewish Committee, the National Jewish Community Relations Council, Temple Emanu-El, and The San Francisco Bulletin. Edward's wife, Cathryn, has been president of the Mount Zion Hospital Auxiliary, and for many years a devoted member. These are just a few of the volunteer services shouldered by the children of Florine and Alice.

In recent times, the pendulum has swung back to the synagogue and temple. My children attended Sunday school with enthusiasm.

Both my sons were bar mitzvah. Susan and John went on to confirmation and post-confirmation classes, and then taught Sunday school. They enjoyed being counselors at Jewish camps. Susan is married to a rabbi whom she met while attending college in Geneva. It was there that she joined Hillel and met and fell in love with Léo Abrami. Two of my children, John and Susan, observe the Sabbath, although their parents, grandparents, and great-grandparents did not. Son John comes home for dinner every Friday night after attending services; he wears a *yarmulke* on his head. He lights the candles, blesses the wine, breaks the bread, and says the prayers. I treasure this weekly ritual that never before existed for me.

Susan and John observe the dietary laws, go to temple regularly, and celebrate the Jewish holidays—not Christian festivals. At present, John is the president of the San Francisco chapter of the Zionist Organization of America, chairman of the Soviet Jewry Commission of the Jewish Community Relations Council, and chairman of the Development Committee of the Bureau of Jewish Education. From 1970 to 1973, John served as the consultant for Adolescent Programs for the Bureau of Jewish Education in Los Angeles and was principal of the religious school of Congregation Beth Shalom in Whittier. John has traveled to Israel several times in his twenty-eight years and is avid to return. In 1972, he spent the summer as the director of the Ulpan of the Los Angeles Bureau of Jewish Education at Meir Shefeya in Israel. John is deeply immersed in and concerned with Jewish affairs, and practices his religion with heart and soul in addition to serving organizations. Of course, Susan and her rabbi husband and their five children practice their religion, too. My oldest granddaughter was bat mitzvah; it was a moving event because her father performed the ceremony. My three grandsons were circumcised in the traditional manner and with festivity. These descriptions of affirming tradition do not pertain to everyone in the family. Liz still stages Easter-egg hunts and Christmas parties for her granddaughter. And although Madeleine has a ceiling-high Christmas tree and festoons her house with Christmas decorations, she serves on the boards of innumerable Jewish organizations and is noted for her great generosity to Jewish causes.

Last Christmas Eve, fifty William Haas descendants celebrated at 2007 Franklin Street, now San Francisco Heritage's headquarters. It was the usual nostalgic gathering of the clan. All members of the family joined in the festivities and delighted in the sparkling tree. There was, of course, a great void: the very essence of 2007—the shining presence of Aunt Alice presiding over all. The party could not and did not pretend to imitate the many Christmases she staged so miraculously. No Santa lumbered down the stairs bellowing his "Ho Ho Ho." There were no gray pearls of fresh caviar inviting us to indulge; there was no Tillie, the longtime rotund German cook, taking smiling bows for her special preparations. Sometimes, a magician was hired to entertain the children. We ladies were the cooks who brought what we fixed at home. Platters of tempting food crowded the golden-oak table: turkeys, ham, a huge wheel of Brie, clusters of stuffed eggs, bowls of crisp salads, casseroles of candied sweet potatoes, mushroom rice, buttered green vegetables, stacks of ginger and anise Christmas cookies, and rich dark chocolate cake. There were speeches, toasts, gifts, and merriment. The family banded together again for the fun and festivity of Christmas without the religious connotations. The celebration succeeded in reviving a treasured echo: the glimmer, the tinsel, and the fragrance of times past.

For Mother's and Aunt Alice's particular class of Jew in San Francisco, the nineteenth century was one of security, propriety, tranquility: one of successful enterprises, affluence, and social amenities. Of course, they felt the brutal repercussions of World War I, but that did not take place until they were grown and in their thirties—and then, it was fought on another continent. They did not live in the midst of guns and destruction. Their homes and their families stood as bulwarks of security. Their world never toppled; it only shook with a scarcely perceptible threat. Even the big earthquake of 1906 seemed to hold off for Mother and Aunt Alice at their very doorsteps as destruction stopped short of Franklin Street. Van Ness Avenue was in shambles, but 2007 and 1735 Franklin Street were scarcely affected. The depression undermined their fortune, but it did not affect the even flow of their comfortable lives. Disasters, tragedies, crumbling of amassed wealth, suicides, insolvencies happened to others; my family simply adjusted to fewer servants and tempered their dinner parties.

Mother and Aunt Alice lived in a cottoned world of security. What could they know of ghettos, iron-fisted militarism, and revolutions that existed for their forefathers a century earlier? What could they know of persecution, these ladies who were so loved and accepted? How could they smell the horror of the ashes of their fellow Jews, thousands of miles removed from isolated San Francisco? The daggers of pain and death could not penetrate their senses, but their hearts were never immune to the suffering of others.

In the late years of the second World War, the Haas sisters gave generous sums of money and wrote affidavits for their fellow Jews living dangerously, dying agonizingly in Germany. They worked for every war cause. No two human beings ever gave more love, kindness, generosity, and humanity than Aunt Alice and Mother. It was the tranquil, protected segment of time in which they were nurtured, followed by long years of relative fulfillment and serenity, which places them in what was often termed "the lost generation." Mother and Aunt Alice were integrated into the cultural world around them, but certainly not socially assimilated, for they never denied their German Jewish origins. Heart and soul, they were American Victorian sisters, raised in the special environment of San Francisco of the late nineteenth century. They were a striking product, an endearing example of their era—unique, rare human beings, never to be again, on whom we look back with love.

Top left: Alice Haas shortly before her wedding, 1909. **Bottom left:** William Haas, 1880s. **Top right:** Florine Haas, circa 1900s. **Bottom right:** Bertha Haas, circa 1880s.

Opposite page, top: William and Bertha at Haas family gathering in Reckendorf, Bavaria (Germany), his hometown, circa 1911. **Middle left:** Young Charles and Alice Haas with cousin Louis Greene (né Greenebaum), 1890s. **Bottom left:** William Haas with grandson Ernest Lilienthal at the Panama-Pacific International Exposition in San Francisco, 1915. **Middle right:** The Haas family ancestral home in Reckendorf, Bavaria, circa 1911. **Bottom right:** William and Bertha Haas in Venice, feeding the pigeons in St. Mark's Square, 1911.

P.P.I.E. SAN FRANCISCO MAY 1915

Two Victorian-Era Houses

<><><><><><><><><><><><><><><><><><><><><><><><><><><><><><><><><><><><><><>

The Haas-Lilienthal House, 2007 Franklin Street

From its first settlement, San Francisco had been a city of cramped streets and constricted building lots. With the westward expansion of the town, 125-foot-wide Van Ness Avenue was laid out to relieve density. Before the destruction of the 1906 earthquake and fire, this grand boulevard had become adorned with large, ostentatious Victorian mansions, while the new district to the west was developing with ample, comfortable, more modest dwellings. 2007 Franklin was one such home.

Residential architecture in the booming San Francisco of the 1870s and '80s was predominantly in the Stick-Eastlake style, inspired in line and ornament by the well-known London furniture designer Sir Charles Eastlake. This popular style was angular and crisp in feeling, with strong vertical emphasis. During the mid '80s, the more exuberant Queen Anne style became prevalent, emphasizing dynamic, asymmetrical compositions: gabled roofs, rounded bay windows, classically derived ornamentation, and featuring a round corner tower topped by a steep conical roof nicknamed a "witch's cap." The Haas-Lilienthal house has deeply shaped moldings, turnings, elaborate pendants, robust fretwork ornamentation, and a picturesque balcony off-center on the third-floor front. Yet in much of the detail, its angularity, and particularly the configuration of the bays over the front porch and on the south wall there appear unmistakable Stick-Eastlake motifs. This synthesis of elements marks the house as a distinctive "transitional style" example. Built in 1886 for William Haas, a wholesale grocer, by architect Peter R. Schmidt, with McCann and Biddell as contractors, the new house gained quick recognition for excellence in a city of many beautiful Victorian homes. Featuring a photograph of the home, the *San Francisco News Letter* of November 19, 1887, remarked, "Beautiful residences have been erected along Franklin Street, but none finer than this one."

Possessing grand scale and opulent material and detail, there is still a remarkable similarity of floor plan between the Haas-Lilienthal house and its more modest Victorian cousins, those standard middle-class row houses that covered the city's hills. Nearly all San Francisco houses of the period have on their first floor a series of three rooms laid out parallel to one long hall along one side of the house. From the formal front parlor one progressed to the second parlor, and then to the dining room with its projecting bay window. Behind the dining room were a breakfast room, pantry, kitchen, and back stairs. The Haas-Lilienthal house exemplifies this arrangement, with refined elaboration and sumptuousness.

The entry hall opens through an archway onto the stair hall, and is encircled by a five-foot dado of golden oak. Simulated leather with a stenciled border extends from the dado to the thirteen-foot-high ceiling, in typical Eastlake fashion. To the left, the front parlor incorporates a mahogany dado, and a "classicizing" cornice, dating this room from a later period, close to 1900. The second parlor appears warmer in its less formal detailing and California redwood woodwork, and boasts a fireplace faced in Numidian red marble from

Egypt, known as the "marble of the Pharaohs." Through the customary sliding "pocket" doors, the dining room is rendered predominantly in golden oak, though the dado here is lesser wood painted to look like oak. This convincing simulation, like that of the entry hall "leather," was a typical device of the era. Here the fireplace facing is of Italian green serpentine marble, and the mantel is carved oak, whose garlands recall those on the exterior of the house. The breakfast room behind the dining room was used by William Haas as a study; no one is positive about the purpose of the floor-to-ceiling window, a unique feature. Immediately after the 1906 catastrophe, the entire first floor was pressed into service for extended office space for his wholesale grocery business, the family having been evacuated to the East Bay as a precaution against further tremors. Next to the breakfast room are the butler's pantry, kitchen, food pantry, and cold room (a space left at outside temperature with an icebox). Most of the kitchen appliances date from the 1920s. The kitchen includes a large marble-topped table for pastry making, and a call system for the servants.

As in most Victorians, the second floor layout corresponds to that of the first floor. The front room was originally the principal bedroom, but was later converted to an informal sitting room. The bay window in this room is brightened by stained-glass panels and nugget-like pieces that add sparkle to the windows. Traditionally the windows were covered with heavy, dark curtains. Connected to the master bedroom is a sunny room used as a bedroom by Bertha Haas's maid. Across the hall, between the master bedroom and its sitting room, is a bright bathroom. The fixtures are of various dates, but the tub and vanity are probably original. A gas burner in the alcove was used for heating curling irons or preparing food for the ill.

Most row houses of the period had flat roofs with no attic story, and sat on brick footings. The larger Haas-Lilienthal house, built to the requirements of a more well-to-do Victorian family, includes a full basement with work and storerooms, laundry room, and a handsome redwood-paneled ballroom, which was completed at the turn of the century. Under the large gabled roof, a full attic contains storage rooms, a spacious children's playroom, and large servants' quarters. A house of this period and lifestyle required a full staff of servants, whose number varied over time, but included at least a cook, a waitress, a maid, a governess, a laundryman, and part-time gardener and chauffeur. This gracious home was constructed in 1886 for the then substantial sum of $18,500, at a time when most houses were being built for $2,000 or less. The original 60 by 137.5–foot lot, valued at $13,000, was also greater than the standard 25- and 30-foot-wide lots into which the city was being parceled. Convinced that the house as built demanded a more appropriate setting than the original lot, in 1898 William Haas purchased an additional lot, to the south, 34 feet and 4 ½ inches wide, to expand the garden-side court. Twenty-nine years later, in 1927, his son-in-law and daughter, Samuel and Alice Haas Lilienthal, built an addition attached to the rear south corner of the original home. This wing, designed by noted architect Gardner Dailey, included garage space and living quarters to accommodate the two young children of her recently deceased brother, Charles William Haas. The addition, now a rental unit, serves as a backdrop for the mature vegetation of the garden. Though sympathetic in elements and proportion to the original, the addition does not try to compete with the main house in grandeur. The original Haas-Lilienthal house thus remains for us to experience much as it appeared when first built: a testament to prosperity and confidence, to be treasured for its rich craftsmanship, noble composition, and family history.

The Bransten House, 1735 Franklin Street

A few blocks south on Franklin Street from the Haas-Lilienthal house stands the later Bransten house, a wedding gift from the William Haases on the occasion of the marriage of their daughter Florine to Edward Bransten. Designed in 1904 by architect Herman Barth, it represents an adaptation of the neo-Georgian style to the narrow, deep lots of San Francisco. This large brick house is entered from the side, at a central hall and staircase, freeing precious street frontage for one grand room with pediment window on the facade.

Like the few other such houses in this style built in Pacific Heights, it represents the return to simpler, almost severe, massing with relatively unadorned window openings. In its materials and detailing it hints at distant American Colonial homes; with the use of brick (rare for California), classical cornice, and balustrade at the roofline, it is a real departure from the Victorian spirit. The house benefits greatly from the rare open space between it and the corner Coleman house. The welcome wide lawn, as well as the Coleman house and the Italianate house around the corner on California Street, owe their fortuitous survival to the foresight of the Bransten family, who acquired these parcels over time to preserve the light and view for their original home. The Branstens remained in the wholesale coffee business. Their MJB company is still based in San Francisco. Here and there, on old buildings San Francisco, the surviving ads for MJB coffee with their enormous question mark and cryptic slogan "Why?" continue to puzzle passersby.

(Invaluable assistance and source materials for this article were provided by The Foundation for San Francisco's Architectural Heritage, now San Francisco Heritage, and its publication *A Victorian Sampler* by Randolph Delehanty.)

ADDENDA

◇◇

Travels with the Sisters—Mother Arrested Again
(as told to me by William Haas Bransten)

In the early 1930s Mother and my brother, William, went to Hono-lulu. There, Mother was intrigued with the coffee plants growing in tropical abundance. How wonderful, she thought, to bring home cof-fee plants as gifts, for they were both beautiful and appropriate for Mother to bestow as the wife of the president of a coffee firm. The United States Department of Agriculture had strict laws forbidding any plant being brought back to the mainland, because of pests or diseases an imported plant might transmit. Nevertheless, Mother, persistent as ever, refused to believe she couldn't take those lovely plants back with her. She inquired of everyone if there wasn't a way. Certainly those lush and tender plants were completely innocent and couldn't harm a living thing. Pronouncing the law "utter nonsense," and unbeknownst to William, she bulldozed a stranger into carrying several plants aboard the *Lurline* ocean liner.

The day came for the *Lurline* to dock. Father and my sister, Alice, went to meet the ship in happy anticipation of the reunion. They watched and waited while every passenger and most of the crew dis-embarked. No sign of Mother or of William! Father, beside himself with worry, made frantic inquiries. He finally learned that Mother and William had been locked into Mother's stateroom. Mother was under arrest and her room was being fumigated. Of course all Mother's precious plants were confiscated. It is possibly the sole time in his life that my father was infuriated with Mother.

The Good Fairy (as told to me by Ernest Reuben Lilienthal)

Aunt Alice insisted upon treating the entire entourage that accompanied her to Las Vegas. Reluctant to accept such generosity, her children reimbursed her. The morning of departure each and every one awakened to find a hundred-dollar bill slipped under their door with a note attached, "From the Blackjack Fairy." That was that! Aunt Alice forever chose to give rather than to receive.

The Accident (as told to me by Madeleine Haas Russell)

One Christmas vacation when Madeleine was attending Smith College, she went to Washington, DC, for the holiday. While perilously groping her way across a busy street, in ice and sleet, a taxicab swerved into her, knocking her down. Fortunately she only suffered bruises. Returning to her hotel, still utterly shaken, she telephoned long distance to Aunt Alice in San Francisco, yearning for comfort and sympathy. Across the miles, Aunt Alice worried solicitously, "Oh, my dear, I do hope your shoes weren't ruined."

Hers Not to Reason Why (as told to me by Frank Sloss)

In the years 1909 to 1921, Alice and Sam's aunt and uncle Judge and Mrs. M.C. Sloss had a summer home in Ross Valley. Traveling to Marin County in those pre-bridge days meant going by ferryboat to Sausalito and then boarding an electric train to one's further destination.

One summer the Slosses were in need of a new automobile tire. In those long-ago years one could purchase a tire only in the big metropolis of San Francisco—not in the backwoods of Ross Valley. Accordingly, Mrs. Sloss had ordered a tire to be delivered to her in Ross. It chanced that at the same time she also had requested a repaired wristwatch to be sent over from Shreve's. Aunt Alice and Uncle Sam were invited to spend a weekend with the Slosses. It was customary then to leave all deliveries for Marin County in the checkroom of the Ferry Building. Mrs. Sloss suggested to Aunt Alice that perhaps she wouldn't mind picking up a package in the checkroom addressed to the Slosses and bringing it along. Mrs. Sloss hadn't thought to stipulate which package. On this Friday morning, Aunt Alice, dressed in her delicate summer best, probably soft voile gown and straw bonnet, left for Ross Valley. Uncle Sam would follow in the late afternoon when Haas Brothers closed. Trooping into the checkroom, Aunt Alice dutifully glanced around. The first thing she spotted was the huge automobile tire. Not noticing the small, compact Shreve's package, she assumed the tire was what her Aunt Hattie wished. She eyed the tire, knowing it would be cumbersome. On the other hand her aunt needed it and had asked her especially to bring "the package" along. Hers not to reason why. Gritting her teeth, Aunt Alice resolutely rolled the bulky tire alongside her. Mrs. Sloss met Aunt Alice at the station in her chauffeured limousine. Aunt Hattie and her chauffer watched astonished as Aunt Alice, dressed in her summer best, staggered off the electric train proudly wheeling the tire as though it were the most natural baggage in the world for a young woman. Aunt Alice was surprised at the shocked reaction with which she was greeted, for, of course, Mrs. Sloss had meant her niece to bring the small Shreve's box. After all, whatever was requested of my Aunt Alice was of necessity accomplished: she thought the tire was what had been requested and so she delivered it.

Tears and Laughter

A close and beloved relative of Mother's and Aunt Alice's had died at far too young an age. The sisters were inconsolable, so deep was their grief. They went to the funeral in a taut state of emotion, equipped with handkerchiefs, prepared to weep copiously. The services took place in the Victorian home of the bereaved family. There, in the flower-bedecked parlor, Aunt Alice and Mother took front-row seats. Surreptitiously Mother glanced around at the many somber mourners. "Alice," Mother whispered, "we must have come to the wrong funeral. I don't see a single soul I know."

Aunt Alice stole a furtive look. "Nor I," she whispered back. With that the sisters doubled over in uncontrollable fits of laughter. They sat through what proved to be the right funeral, wracked with deep grief, profound embarrassment—and the giggles.

AFTERWORD

◇◇

Our mother would have been thrilled by the restoration of the Haas-Lilienthal house and by the reissue of her charming book. The National Trust for Historic Preservation has declared the house a "National Treasure." This book also is a literary treasure trove, providing us a glimpse of an earlier era and family life inside the four walls of this special Victorian mansion.

Mom loved to write. Her fondest memories, of her family and the joyous early years of her life, inspired her book. The Haas-Lilienthal-Bransten families lived within blocks of each other. They shared day-to-day activities, holidays, vacations, and the joy of a large and close-knit family. While writing this book our mother was able to make the Haas sisters live again in the minds and hearts of all who embrace those special times in San Francisco.

In the final chapter of the book, our mother mentions the trend in succeeding generations to return to the observant practice of Judaism. This trend has continued and grown to the point that several of her grandchildren actively practice their faith, and feel very connected to *Eretz* (the land of) Israel. Other descendants are community, synagogue, and philanthropic leaders. The core and extended family continue to gather at the house every Christmas Eve, and recall with love their ancestors, the beloved "Haas Sisters of Franklin Street."

As visitors enjoy their time in the Haas-Lilienthal house, they will learn about the architecture and history of a splendid Queen Anne Victorian. How fortunate we are that by sharing the stories in this book the dynamic of the family will once again come to life. Our entire extended family has participated in the restoration of the house and in the updating and reissuing of this volume. William and Bertha Haas, their children Florine, Charles, and Alice, and those of us in the succeeding generations rejoice that this part of our history will survive for years to come.

—Susan Rothmann Seeley, William E.G. Rothmann,

and John F. Rothmann, 2017

John, Susan, and William Rothmann, circa 1951.

ABOUT THE AUTHOR

Frances Bransten Rothmann (1914–1984) was born and raised in San Francisco. Educated in local schools and at Scripps College in Claremont, California, she graduated from Barnard College in 1937. In 1938 she married Hans Rothmann, a German-born physician. She had three children and nine grandchildren. As a widow, she studied at the Fromm Institute, University of San Francisco, and enjoyed freelance writing.

Since 1971, San Francisco Heritage, or "Heritage," has been leading the civic discussion about the compatibility of rapid change with protecting our past. Built on its activist underpinnings, Heritage has been instrumental in establishing the preservation protections that have allowed San Francisco to evolve and flourish while retaining its unique character. Heritage is a nonprofit 501(c)(3) membership organization with a mission to preserve and enhance San Francisco's unique architectural and cultural identity.

In 1973, Heritage was entrusted with caring for the Haas-Lilienthal house, a pristine 1886 Victorian that was home to "The Haas Sisters of Franklin Street." Today the house serves many functions: as a house museum, a popular event venue, and as Heritage's administrative offices. Through a variety of activities including Heritage Hikes for schoolchildren, the house is the centerpiece of Heritage's education program and has become a powerful exemplar of responsible stewardship.

In 2017, Heritage successfully completed the $4.3 million Campaign for San Francisco Heritage/Haas-Lilienthal House. This book is dedicated to the myriad foundations and individual donors whose generous support helped secure and restore this landmark building, and thereby continue to ensure the vigor and utility of the historic-preservation movement in San Francisco.

sfheritage.org

haas-lilienthalhouse.org

HEYDAY

into California

ABOUT HEYDAY

Heyday is an independent, nonprofit publisher and unique cultural institution. We promote widespread awareness and celebration of California's many cultures, landscapes, and boundary-breaking ideas. Through our well-crafted books, public events, and innovative outreach programs we are building a vibrant community of readers, writers, and thinkers.

THANK YOU

It takes the collective effort of many to create a thriving literary culture. We are thankful to all the thoughtful people we have the privilege to engage with. Cheers to our writers, artists, editors, storytellers, designers, printers, bookstores, critics, cultural organizations, readers, and book lovers everywhere!

We are especially grateful for the generous funding we've received for our publications and programs during the past year from foundations and hundreds of individual donors. Major supporters include:

Anonymous (2); Arkay Foundation; John Atwood, in memory of Jeanne Carevic; Judith and Phillip Auth; Judy Avery; Richard and Rickie Ann Baum; Randy Bayard; BayTree Fund; Jean and Fred Berensmeier; Nancy Bertelsen; Edwin Blue; Philip and Jamie Bowles; Beatrice Bowles; Peter Boyer and Terry Gamble Boyer; Brandt-Hawley Law Group; John Briscoe; California Humanities; California State Library; The Campbell Foundation; John and Nancy Cassidy; The Christensen Fund; The City of Berkeley; Lawrence Crooks; Chris Desser and Kirk Marckwald; Steven Dinkelspiel; Frances Dinkelspiel and Gary Wayne; The Roy and Patricia Disney Family Foundation; Tim Disney; Patricia Dixon; Gayle Embrey; Richard and Gretchen Evans; Federated Indians of Graton Rancheria; Megan Fletcher, in honor of J.K. Dineen; Patrick Golden and Susan Overhauser; Wanda

GETTING INVOLVED

To learn more about our publications, events, and other ways you can participate, please visit www.heydaybooks.com.